To my wife, Linda, who encouraged me,
and to my three children: Guild, Justin, and Megan

THE
Adventure
OF
Retirement

IT'S ABOUT MORE THAN JUST MONEY

Guild A. Fetridge

 Prometheus Books

59 John Glenn Drive
Amherst, NewYork 14228-2197

Published 1994 by Prometheus Books

Library of Congress Cataloging-in-Publication Data

Fetridge, Guild A.
    The adventure of retirement : it's about more than just money / Guild A. Fetridge.
        p.   cm.
    Includes bibliographical references.
    ISBN 0-87975-921-6 (alk. paper : cloth)
    ISBN 0-87975-941-0 (alk. paper : paper)
    1. Retirement—United States—Planning. I. Title.
HQ1064.U5F45   1994
646.7'9—dc20   94-19656
                                                                         CIP

Printed in the United States of America on acid-free paper.

Contents

Foreword

"Great retirements don't just happen, they are planned. They require making choices and developing plans."*

Ever wonder why the word "retirement" is still being used to describe what happens when people disengage from their careers and jobs? "To retire" means to retreat, to depart from, to quit. It can also mean to surrender or abandon; to be obscure, secluded, or sequestered.

I spend a lot of time traveling throughout the United States and Canada as a professional speaker and workshop leader doing presentations to a large cross-section of companies as well as professional and trade associations. I may do a one- or two-day workshop, for example, at a large chemical or paper and pulp processing company plant in the Southeast or Northwest for a group of employees and their spouses. Or I might deliver a one-hour keynote presentation to the general membership of a national education organization or a "partners" (spouse or guest) program for a banker's group. A lot of the material for these programs comes from my research over the past sixteen years as well as research done by others. These presentations, sometimes referred to as "life planning," explore a wide variety of important retirement preparation and postretirement issues from the behavioral, emotional, psychological, social, lifestyle, and financial areas

---

*Author's note: The epigraphs to each chapter have been taken from the comments of retired people who participated in my research throughout the years.

9

to the unique problems that adult children and other family members may face in helping elders.

Nearly one million Americans retire each year, and that number will nearly double when the baby boomers (those born between 1946 and 1964) begin to retire around the year 2011. These programs are important because they provide a great deal of information and practical strategies about planning for the future before people retire.

Sometimes I ask the people attending my seminars what thoughts and images first come to mind when they consider the word "retired." Many answer, believe it or not, "old-fashioned," "eccentric," "bad-tempered," "bossy," "worn out," "no spring chicken," "out of touch," "incapacitated," "you are in the slow lane and pull off to the side of the road," and so on.

This is certainly not what most people today think of when retirement comes to mind, or at least it shouldn't be. Of course, many did think this way years ago. It was more appropriate to look on retirement as rare or eccentric when life expectancy was shorter than it is today. Early in this century, people worked until they were no longer able to; they became frail and incapacitated, and then they died.

It is important to recognize that today a considerable period of time can be spent in retirement. Life expectancy has increased by more than twenty-five years during the twentieth century and is steadily rising from 46.3 years (in 1900) to 75.5 years today. We are seeing the continuation of adult activity into one's eighties and even nineties, twenty-five to thirty-five years past retirement age. This is no small part of a person's life and it should not be relegated to feelings of dependence and looking back.

This phase of life can be just as challenging, interesting, and rewarding as the other two major phases of maturity: 1) growing up (physically, emotionally, and intellectually) and 2) achieving adult independence through work and choosing a spouse or significant other. In retirement we can learn, explore, and develop new interests about which we may have been previously unaware. After all, education is continuous. Retirement also offers many new opportunities to earn money, as I will discuss later.

We know that many of today's older Americans are high achievers, innovators, and pioneers; they are trendsetters with whom others identify positively. The euphemisms "senior citizen" and "golden ager" no longer mean "has beens" to many of today's retirees, who often consider themselves active and fully engaged. They take advantage of the unlimited options and choices they have in this new phase of their lives. These are not the typical stereotypes that people express when asked what thoughts the word "retired" evokes; still, the stereotypes linger, such as those of people, their memory failing, sitting and doing nothing and falling asleep frequently; those with sciatica and a broken hip, lack of stamina, and wheezing and coughing a lot; those portrayed in television commercials scrubbing their dentures, taking laxatives and painkillers; lonely people; people in large busloads traveling to Atlantic City; or those who often repeat themselves and are surly and obstinate. Take your pick. These stereotypes are more like myths today.

I believe that the word "retirement" conveys an erroneous image and reinforces for many people a negative stereotype of this new phase of life. The word itself should be "retired." Let's call it "renewal," "new midlife," "the next chapter" . . . anything but retirement. Pick the term or phrase that best suits how you envision your life after leaving your career.

It is important to ask: What are the challenges I will face in the years ahead? What are the problems I will meet? What kind of life will be most rewarding for me, the most useful for society, and the most helpful for my friends and family?

There is more to retirement than perfecting a golf swing, taking that Jamaican cruise you always promised yourself, or finally having the time to do all those odd jobs around the house. It can represent for some an endless array of business opportunities, from opening an independent consulting firm to launching a whole new career. For others, it's a personal rebirth, a time to remarry or to rediscover longtime spouses and fall in love all over again. Still others broaden their horizons through involvement with the arts, discovering new talents and skills in crafts they never before had the opportunity to try. After a lifetime of taking from society and our culture, there comes a time for many to reinvest and give back through volunteer work. Returning to the classroom to acquire new skills or knowledge just because it's stimulating and exciting has a meaningful impact on many retirees. Others will discover the exhilaration of travel while some find unlimited enjoyment in such simple pleasures as learning to square dance or going bird watching.

While there are people who carefully plan what they will do at the end of their career, others don't have any clear ideas, while still others will entirely revise their blueprints in the midst of coming to grips with their post-career lifestyle and the many new choices facing them. Many who retire say, "I had all these fun extracurricular activities, but I didn't have a feeling of satisfaction, of being useful, or feeling needed as I did when I was working."

Deciding how to use time effectively and learning to successfully adjust to other key aspects of retirement is a relatively recent problem for many because retirement itself is a comparatively new phenomenon in American society. We have always had rules and norms for other stages of life, and guidelines for our other roles, but not for retirement. The reasons are fairly obvious.

When this century began, people had to work much longer than they do today. In 1900, steel workers, for example, were on the job twelve hours a day, seven days a week, fifty-two weeks a year. It was not all that much different for miners, factory workers, and many other types of employment. The average life expectancy then was 46.3 years, and the average employee was bound by economic necessity to stay on the job until death or disablement. There were no pensions or social security at this time; all "retirement" meant was "not working," and therefore it was associated with poverty. It was a time of withdrawal, an end to a productive life.

Since the Social Security Act of 1935 had begun to provide a source of retirement income for the bulk of the nation's workers, and industry had started to offer pensions to a sizable segment of the working population during World War II, retirement became a realistic concept by mid-century. Even then, however, it didn't hold a lot of promise for the average employee since the income of most retirees was pitifully low. Unions impacted the evolution of retirement at this time and made the promise of retirement with dignity a potential reality for millions of workers through a flood of collectively bargained pension plans. Since the 1950s, a comfortable retirement has become possible for more and more Americans. With the opportunities people now have to retire at younger ages, with greater life expectancy, increased pay scales, and a variety of employee and employer savings plans, retirement has become a commonplace rather than the rarity it once was.

Even so, most Americans have not been properly prepared for retirement. We can spend a quarter of our lives preparing for a career, but then do very little organizing for the period afterward. Imagine yourself filling eight to ten hours a day, every day, for the next three decades and adjusting to the new change of pace! Can you do it? Of course! During your career work and home were separate worlds. Will your retirement change your marital behavior or your relationship with your partner? Perhaps, but doesn't that help keep life interesting? Will you eventually fall into a debilitating routine of waking, eating, sleeping, and watching television? Not necessarily. At some point in retirement will you use a certain age, seventy for example, to calibrate your purpose and worth in life, e.g., that you're "old" now and it's time to "wind down" living? Some people do, but there's no reason to.

What an adventure lies ahead!

1

"So How's Retirement?"

"Do not retire for the wrong reasons, but when you do, think and approach it with a positive and decisive attitude. Be prepared to work at making retirement a success with the same effort that you did to making your working career successful."

"Retirement is like being in heaven but still being alive."

"Retirement is the ugliest word in the language." Ernest Hemingway said that. I'm not exactly sure what he meant by that statement but it was probably reflective of a negative attitude toward retirement. Some of us have only read something about retirement or talked with someone who is retired. Most of us have had some personal experience with the subject when parents or grandparents retired. Perhaps their retirement experiences helped form your own attitudes and expectations about what retirement will be like for you.

Try to gauge your present feelings toward retirement by answering "true" or "false" to each of the following statements:

1. Retirement will work itself out one way or another; there's no need to go through the process of planning ahead.
   True ( ) False ( )
2. If people are successful in their jobs and careers, then it seems only logical that their retirement will also be successful.
   True ( ) False ( )

3. Going from a life of full-time productive work to one of retirement is not a difficult transition.
   True ( ) False ( )
4. Most people who are financially secure are usually satisfied in retirement.
   True ( ) False ( )
5. About a third of retired Americans today would still like to be working.
   True ( ) False ( )

The answer to statements 1 through 4 is false; the answer to statement 5 is true.

If you answered two or more statements incorrectly, you may need to carefully reconsider your views on retirement.

Fifteen years ago, while in charge of personnel working with a major international sales and marketing company, I organized a retirees' day. The company had made some changes in the pension plan and, as with all such alterations, my department was required to inform the retirees. While these people could have been notified by formal letter, it seemed more appropriate, more personal, to do it directly. There were other reasons for wanting to have a retirees' day. Many current employees often asked about former coworkers. Some would ask, "Have you heard how David Murray is doing now that he's retired?" or "It certainly is quiet in the Marketing Department since Sharon retired. I wish she would stop in and say hello." There seem to be some ambivalent feelings when people retire after working for a company for many years. They are often viewed as part of the organization, not merely as employees or coworkers; we get used to them and we miss them, although we are also envious when they retire.

Another reason to have a retirees' day is that retired employees are wonderful public relations ambassadors for the company. Most people who retire often talk about where they have spent a substantial portion of their life, namely on the job. If such comments are positive, the benefits to the company can be significant.

The all-day program was certainly a success, and had an important positive impact on the company's employee relations. It demonstrated to former workers that the company really cared and that it was concerned about them, not only when they were contributing to the organization but now that they had left as well. After conveying the pension changes to the retirees, there was a lunch buffet, a tour of some new facility changes, and an opportunity for the retired coworkers to say "hello" to former colleagues. During that day, while I talked with the retired employees and their spouses (who were also invited), I could tell something wasn't quite right. Many admitted that their retirement experience was less than they had expected. The following remarks were not uncommon: "Retirement isn't what I expected"; "It's a bit disappointing"; "Perhaps I should have continued working"; "Retirement is all right, I guess, if you consider sleeping and reading exciting"; "It took me only nine months to do everything I'd been planning for the last thirty-five years. What am I going to do now for the next twenty-five?" and "My wife complains about me being home so much."

Some retirees I talked with seemed to thoroughly enjoy their retirement; here are a few examples:

Jim retired from his job six years ago and his three children say he is hard to locate and they almost need an appointment to see him. "I'm doing all the things I promised myself I would do," Jim says. He buys a home needing repair in a certain town, repairs and makes improvements on it, then sells it for a good profit. He does this every two years and has the enjoyment of living in different locations and making new friends.

Debbie and her husband turned their three extra bedrooms into rooms for tourists and business travelers, and now operate a bed and breakfast. They told me, "After our children moved out and got on with their own lives, our house was too large for two people."

Pamela and Dick had just returned from Botswana in Africa as Peace Corps volunteers, and planned to be on another assignment within six months. "Because older people are revered in most developing countries, older volunteers immediately command a respect it might take a younger person a year to earn," Pamela and Dick told me. (People over fifty-five make up about 10 percent of current Peace Corps volunteers.)

Bill spends three mornings each week at a local hospital for children as a volunteer holding babies who have been abandoned or who have parents deemed unfit to care for them. "I give these special infants something that even the most sophisticated medical equipment cannot duplicate: love," Bill says. It reminds him of when he held his own children. Bill became a volunteer for this program, called TLC (Tender Loving Care), two years ago. It is also sometimes called The Lap Parents program.

Susan, age seventy, works six months each year as a swimming instructor at a camp for older adults. "I'm too young and healthy to retire and not work. I enjoy it because it keeps me busy and healthy."

However, over half the people I talked to were not very enthusiastic about their retirements thus far. This was certainly a shock for me. How could so many people invest time in their careers, devote years of their lives and substantial amounts of money to educate and prepare themselves, and work years reaching career goals, only to find all their efforts culminating in disappointment? It seemed to me that it should be different: retirement should be a delightful, exciting, and productive part of life. I expected the group to enthusiastically view retirement as a new beginning filled with opportunities, challenges, and adventure. Instead, many were inactive and lonely, with unmet expectations, regrets, and even anger. Here are a few examples:

Bernard, who had been retired for six years, missed working and said he should not have retired when he did, although at the time he thought it was a good idea. "I belong to a couple of country clubs, one in Naples, Florida, and one in Purchase, New York. There are lots of retirees there," he said. "They all seem miserable after the first few months of retirement and we're all asking how we can become active again."

John had been retired for three years, but his wife continued to work. She had a secure job and was reluctant to give it up, saying, "It gives me a bit of economic independence and keeps me connected to the outside world." John, who did little more than occasionally work around the yard, had fallen into a debilitating routine of eating, sleeping, and watching television.

Frank and Evelyn had bought a home in a retirement community in Arizona. After becoming permanent residents they soon realized they had made a mistake in confining most of their contacts to older people. They missed the stimulation of being able to mix with and talk to people of all ages.

Richard said that his minister told him the biggest problem he found among retirees, especially men, was alcoholism. Richard said he was no exception. He had begun drinking heavily almost daily shortly following his retirement. "I took early retirement and was not mentally or spiritually prepared for the change in lifestyle. No one pays attention to me and the lack of opportunities to meet other people has been disconcerting. We never know what tomorrow brings, but for me it will bring nothing!"

These reflections on retirement are more than fifteen years old, yet they sound as apt and poignant now as they did then. I have done considerable research since then and have learned a great deal. That early experience sparked my curiosity and created the desire to begin educating people about the realities of retirement and how to have a long, positive post-employment experience.

2

The Illusion of Leisure as a Way of Life

"Those who appear to be unhappy had no plans for retirement and are really homebound to the chair and the television. They are very reluctant to participate in outside activities and appear unwilling to try. During their active years, their job was their main activity."

"We established our priorities for retirement and built our plan accordingly. We stay on the move—a new town, new friends—with life in an RV moving every two or three weeks."

George Bernard Shaw wrote, "A perpetual holiday is a working definition of hell," and the Greek playwright Sophocles said, "A purposeless leisure breeds nothing good." Today, many retired people cannot feel content unless they are actively doing something. What is more, this something has to lend some purpose to their lives. As a prelude to this chapter, respond to the following statements, which may give you an idea of how you view leisure as a component of retirement. Some people who had fixed ideas about leisure discovered their point of view changing during retirement.

1. Total leisure in retirement is a selfish way to live, without concern or compassion for others.
   True ( ) False ( )
2. Studies show that over half of retired men and women say they get more satisfaction from work than leisure during retirement.
   True ( ) False ( )

3. Leisure can be a prime ingredient in a satisfying, healthful, and well-balanced retirement life.
   True ( ) False ( )
4. Hobbies and related activities are good replacements for the satisfaction of work.
   True ( ) False ( )
5. Your greatest gift to yourself is time alone.
   True ( ) False ( )

The answer to statement 1 is false; statements 2 and 3 are true; statements 4 and 5 can be either true or false, depending on your preferences.

During a recent health club workout, I ran into an acquaintance who had retired about a year ago. He had been in the education field his whole life and had spent the last twelve years as principal of a local high school. But he wasn't happy that day. In fact, he was furious. He was frustrated over the fact that, having spent thirty-five years educating himself, improving his skills, working long hours, and always trying to do the best job possible, it had come to this: a life of boredom.

"Why did I do all that?" he asked. "For what?" Then he answered his own question: "Certainly not to play golf or do ceramics! But you know, that's just what I'm doing. The days fly by in a blur; I'm getting very good at just doing nothing and I'm astonished at how quickly nothing happens."

While doing nothing may seem a welcome change at times when stress levels run high, my friend is an excellent example of the many people for whom retirement turns into bewilderment, tedium, frustration, and loneliness.

Most of us don't know what retirement is really like. We try to imagine ourselves in retirement, but often this is a fantasy built on television and magazine advertisements showing a smiling couple riding a golf cart on the fairway, or a loving couple walking hand-in-hand at the water's edge. Everyone is well-dressed and engaged in some pleasurable leisure activity. Too many of us think about retirement without doing any serious, objective planning.

I asked my friend that day what advance planning for retirement he had done. He answered, "I've been carefully managing my finances for twenty years, I should be all right." Like most people, he thought of retirement planning *only* in financial terms, of *saving enough money*.

I asked him what other planning he had done. He said that when he and his wife had discussed retirement, they had both agreed there was "plenty of time" to find a satisfying purpose after he retired. When this didn't happen, he was disappointed, frustrated, and angry.

Then there was John, another friend, who retired a number of years ago. He visited his old company occasionally and many of the workers envied him. His retirement was working perfectly, he said. He was doing all the things he had always wanted to do, playing golf, having cocktails in the afternoon, traveling, fishing. He was always busy.

I later discovered that John wasn't doing any of these things. He spent most of his time at home watching game shows and soap operas on television. The farthest he traveled was to the movies and the grocery store. John was perpetuating the myth of the carefree retiree by emphasizing the illusions about retirement rather than the realities. He wanted to be envied and to demonstrate that he was in control of his life, just as when he was at work.

Some people view retirement as a paid vacation for the rest of their lives. They mention all the things they haven't been able to do and will now have time for. After all, they have forty thousand to sixty thousand hours of free time ahead of them. What usually happens, however, is that somewhere between the sixth and fifteenth month of retirement, they begin to wonder what else there is. The long trip they planned is finished, the attic and garage have been put in order, visits have been made to all the relatives, the house repairs have all been taken care of, the stacks of *National Geographic* magazines are now read, and all those pictures of past vacations are safely tucked away in albums in chronological order. Even all the pictures of the children growing up have been made into separate albums; one for each of the children. Now what? For many, it's a routine of golf, fishing, and a variety of other leisure activities.

While hobbies and recreational activities may entertain, amuse, and interest people, they often do not satisfy and stimulate. They do not provide the intellectual satisfaction and adrenalin flow many people need. There is nothing wrong with hobbies and leisure activities. Some people find them perfectly appropriate and actually build the remainder of their lives around such activities. For many others, however, time consumed by one diversion after another seems too trivial a way to use the freedom that retirement brings, particularly when we consider the long, hard years of struggle it has taken to achieve the free time afforded us in later life.

Many people find pastimes such as gardening, fishing, or golfing, once considered much-anticipated pleasures, now onerous and laborious when they become almost primary vocations. "If I see another golf ball, I'll . . . !" one retired gentleman remarked to me. Another retiree wrote recently during a research project I was conducting, "I cannot emphasize too strongly the need to carefully plan, well in advance, for a busy and productive new phase of life. Most retirees won't admit it but they are bored with inactivity, let down by the loss of their positions at work, and often unable to handle their instant invisibility."

Here are some additional comments from retirees:

"It is nice to be able to relax and do some of the things during retirement that you wanted to do and could not do before: play more golf, read, travel and visit friends. We have been to New England, Virginia, and Florida. Something to pass on to others—after you get caught up with all the odd jobs and hobbies, which takes two to four months, then time drags. I would prefer to work a few hours a day or something to fill my day. The other letdown is when you leave a very responsible job and then retire, you have nothing to fill the void. No one asks for advice, few calls—you are a nobody. Perhaps not quite that bad, but something a person should prepare for."

"It is important to plan ahead for enjoyable and meaningful activity of all kinds, such as joining clubs prior to retirement and accepting leadership roles in the community. This prevents the sudden letdown after retirement. It worked for me."

"I regret that I did not volunteer for service in a hospital or similar type of activity. I didn't even join any organization after I retired. After a few years of just relaxing, but accomplishing nothing, I didn't seem to have the will or the energy to find something worthwhile. Now more time has passed and I'm too old to begin something new."

"When I first retired I enjoyed playing golf in Florida. After doing that for four months, I realized how narrow-sighted I had been."

"There was no definite time for me to retire. I just realized one day that the time had come. I didn't plan at all because I thought that whatever happened would be more of a surprise—but the real surprise was that *nothing happened.* I used to say what you don't do today can be done tomorrow, except there was nothing to do and that was my fault."

3

Gerontophobia

"At eighty-seven, I was too young to take to the rocking chair. Be proud of your age. Regardless of your age, you can still make an imprint."

"My brain has gotten soft and with every breath, I'm making an old person. It's time to wrap things up; grow a few tomatoes."

Most people don't want to get old. Many seem to do everything possible to avoid it, while to others age does not matter at all. I know people in their eighties who feel they have no interests in common with "old people." How do you feel about getting older? Perhaps you will find out by responding "true" or "false" to these statements:

1. Old age begins at age sixty-five.
   True ( ) False ( )
2. As the body ages, a person's intelligence quotient drops, memory weakens, and the ability to learn decreases.
   True ( ) False ( )
3. If you are smart when you are young, you will be smart when you are old.
   True ( ) False ( )
4. Adaptability decreases with increased chronological age; in other words, most older people tend to be set in their ways.
   True ( ) False ( )

5. Most old people are mentally competent.
   True ( ) False ( )

Statements 1, 2, and 4 are false; statements 3 and 5 are true.

Preretirement planning tends to be focused predominantly on financial issues. Money is certainly important, but only as a "ticket" of sorts: it pays for the ride, but it is the ride, not necessarily the money, that has meaning. In a culture that is focused on financial survival at the expense of life itself, many people are unaware of and unprepared for the emotional, psychological, social, and physical aspects of retirement. The nonfinancial elements are often as important as, if not more significant than, economic security. For some people retirement becomes a major life change. It isn't easy to leave full-time productive work life, whether it's that of a dedicated homemaker, a service provider, a small business owner, or a corporate executive. Retirement can require significant adjustments.

Throughout my travels, I have opportunities to meet and talk with many retirees. In many cases, as these folks get older their behavior changes and they begin to act like "old people," especially with regard to their feelings and attitudes about getting older. It isn't necessary for people to act that way, although my research reveals a variety of reasons why people do. For example, some retirees feel as though they are a minority in the overall population. I frequently hear, "I look around and it seems almost everyone else is younger." Others feel they need to make some changes and adjustments, and acting older seems appropriate because they think other people expect it: "Well, I'm at *that age,* so I might as well act the part," is a typical comment. In my experience a lot of older people feel that certain acts are no longer appropriate: having a lot of energy and vivacity, being spontaneous, showing affection in public, engaging in sports thought to be for younger people, flirting or having an active sex life, enjoying rock music, going to school, and going out alone are some examples. There are those who feel less confident or not as self-assured as they once were, while others begin to feel irrelevant, obsolete or "rudderless" because they aren't working anymore and perhaps are less social than they were prior to retiring. A person's perspective influences whether he or she is enthusiastic about the second half of life. One person sees laugh lines while another finds only wrinkles. Many people accept that growing older means a decrease in physical and personal attractiveness as well as a loss of vitality and sex appeal. Yet youthfulness, vitality, and sex appeal are largely qualities of spirit, not the special domain of a particular age.

According to gerontologists (those who study normal aging) *gerontophobia* is the fear of aging, an obsessive concern about getting older. This fear pervades many people's thoughts and actions and is made up of a series of negative ideas and misconceptions about what it means to grow older. Here are just a few examples:

1. *Learning ability declines with age.* In reality, evidence shows that learning ability, intelligence, memory, and motivation don't fail as people get older. Rather than decreasing, creativity actually improves with age. Vernon H. Mark, M.D., former chief of neurosurgical services at the Harvard Medical School and coauthor with Jeffrey P. Mark, M.S., of the book *Brain Power,* reports that applied skills such as law, medicine, engineering, architecture, and the like do not deteriorate with age. In fact, areas that depend on interpretation, such as art, music, and drama, are enhanced as judgment and wisdom deepen. The ability to speak and write also is enhanced from age fifty to seventy.

2. *In the work setting, younger people work more effectively.* The truth is that with most occupations, productivity levels remain fixed or may even increase with age. Physical stamina and dexterity do decline with age, but other factors have a major influence on productivity, such as concentration on the job, habits, behavior, and motivation.

3. *Older people are set in their ways.* Studies have shown that a younger person can be as strong-willed and inflexible as an older one. Adaptability has been proven to be unrelated to chronological age.

4. *Older people are not interested in romance and most are asexual.* How about this: Recently a progressive nursing home, responding to behaviors they noticed in their elderly residents, opened a "privacy room" for patients who wished to engage in some form of sexual intimacy. Several weeks later it was closed down! Staff and patients had opened it; middle-aged children of the patients closed it. This true anecdote is reminiscent of people's feelings when, as children, they found out that their parents were having sex. Romantic and sexual feelings are very much part of the total range of behaviors in older people. A survey

published in 1990 in the medical journal *Archives of Medicine* suggests that romance and sexual activity are alive and well in the over-sixty crowd. Further, a recent survey of eight hundred men and women across the United States revealed that even the most favorable previous analysis of sex and sexuality in men and women over sixty has been inaccurate. Marcella Bakur Weiner, Ed.D., author of *Sex and Sexuality in the Mature Years,* reports that almost all the subjects, 97.1 percent, stated they were interested in sex. Even among those over eighty, 93.4 percent reported a continuing interest in sex.

Some people will create artificial situations that prevent them from considering the wonderful options and exciting opportunities available in life. A person may say, "At my age and the way I feel, I'm just going to take it easy and stay home. I can't expect any interesting or exciting things to happen to me now." And, of course, nothing ever does.

Case histories and studies have shown how the image we create for ourselves affects the total person. If people think of those over sixty as enfeebled and doddering, what will their minds make of their bodies when they arrive at that age? Precisely that! According to C. Norman Shealy, a former neurosurgeon who now practices holistic medicine, "Most people can determine their own date of death." What a person believes will occur when he or she is older can prove to be a self-fulfilling forecast. Our expectations can mold our future.

We are as young or as old as we make ourselves feel, and our view of life, either optimistic or pessimistic, can affect general health and life expectancy. We have all heard of terminally ill patients who dejectedly accept their fate and soon die, and of others who vow to fight and actually live longer. What of those cheerful and assured individuals who achieve very difficult tasks and overcome unbelievable obstacles, as compared to those who regularly emphasize the negative and expect the worst? Admittedly, anecdotes are not proof; however, there has been some noteworthy evidence recently showing that how people account for the good and bad occurrences in life affects their behavior, their health, and even their longevity.

Noted research psychologist and psychotherapist Martin Seligman, of the University of Pennsylvania, writes in his book *Learned Optimism* how many can train themselves to be optimistic and thereby healthier through their "explanatory style." Seligman describes "explanatory style" as our way of accounting for the good and bad events of our lives.

Pessimists attribute bad events, such as the loss of a job or a divorce, to reasons that are long-lasting or permanent, that are pervasive and affect everything they do, and that are their own fault. Optimists see the causes of such events as temporary; limited to the present case; and the result of circumstances, bad luck, or other people's actions. A pessimist sees success in a career, a romance, or in friendships as the result of luck. An optimist views such success as the result of his or her own efforts and ability.

Our explanatory style can affect our health and longevity. A pessimistic explanatory style appears to depress or weaken the body's immune system, while an optimistic style improves or strengthens it. The evidence is based on a 1989 study done at Yale University, which reviewed a sample of forty people between the ages of sixty-two and eighty-two with no illness or physical conditions that would affect their immune systems. These people were interviewed several times during a two-year period, and once each year their blood was analyzed for T-cell levels (an indicator of the immune system's response to challenge from a virus or disease). The study showed an impressive relationship between pessimistic explanatory style and the body's reduced immune response. In other words, pessimism seems to undermine the immune system. This occurs because when a person becomes depressed, is pessimistic, or is the victim of some misfortune, the brain produces fewer catecholamines, which are important brain neurotransmitters. When these neurotransmitters decrease, it allows the production of endorphins, a neurohormone, to increase. When this occurs the body's immune system has a tendency to shut down.

Other researchers are also finding more evidence of the link between the mind and health. The October 1993 issue of the *AARP Bulletin,* put out by the American Association of Retired Persons, referred to psychiatrist George F. Solomon, of the University of California at Los Angeles, who said: "The mind and body cannot be separated. The mind is the brain, and the brain is part of the body. The brain regulates and influences many physiological functions, including immunity. Mental and physical well-being are inextricably intertwined." Solomon has spent twenty-five years delving into the biological mechanisms by which emotions, stress, and behavior affect resistance to disease: "We have studied people with a variety of illnesses, and people with very good coping skills tend to have a greater speed of recovery."

The common assumption is that a retired or an old person should look, act, and live a certain way. The word "old" has a *deficit orientation* to most people, referring to limitations rather than the fullness and experience of life. Older people are not worn out but seasoned, not out of date but contemporary and continuing to learn, not willing to be inactive but open to a more flexible and productive life. They have managed and coped quite well before, so why not now and on into the future?

People need to confront aging in a healthy way; to learn to become not simply old people but societal elders, those whose remaining time on earth is not a burden to be borne but a source of wisdom and a valuable resource. It's time to redefine old age in a way that matches the style and tempo of the time in which we live. Aging isn't a problem to be mastered but a challenge to live meaningfully.

4

An Extra Eight Hours a Day, Every Day

"The sudden lack of responsibility created a psychological void that, if not corrected, would become a problem. I notice that some other retirees have trouble adjusting to the fact that they are no longer the center of issues, as they were in their jobs. It seems to be very difficult for some to adjust to being so active one day and not the next."

"Have a well-conceived game plan in place ready to be promptly implemented upon leaving the job for retirement. Be certain it contains specifics. It isn't good enough to say, 'I'm going to travel, play more golf, and look around for some part-time work.' "

The two schedules on the following pages will illustrate to the preretiree how much time will really be available in retirement. Now would be a good time to complete these schedules.

Both forms have a 6 A.M. to 11:30 P.M. time scale in thirty-minute intervals for one week. Complete figure 1 with your current weekly schedule (using abbreviations since the space on the form is limited). This should be easy because most of it will revolve around the eight to twelve hours spent working and, perhaps, commuting to and from work.

Next, do your best to fill out figure 2 with an intended postretirement schedule. Keep in mind that this schedule would take effect after the novelty of retirement has subsided and after the initial postretirement activities, which aren't part of the regular routine, are completed. Compare the amount of unfilled time you have to your preretirement schedule.

Figure 1
Preretirement Weekly Planner

	SUN	MON	TUE	WED	THU	FRI	SAT
6:00–6:30 A.M.							
6:30–7:00							
7:00–7:30							
7:30–8:00							
8:00–8:30							
8:30–9:00							
9:00–9:30							
9:30–10:00							
10:00–10:30							
10:30–11:00							
11:00–11:30							
11:30–Noon							
Noon–12:30 P.M.							
12:30–1:00							
1:00–1:30							
1:30–2:00							
2:00–2:30							
2:30–3:00							
3:00–3:30							
3:30–4:00							
4:00–4:30							
4:30–5:00							
5:00–5:30							
5:30–6:00							
6:00–6:30							
6:30–7:00							
7:00–7:30							
7:30–8:00							
8:00–8:30							
8:30–9:00							
9:00–9:30							
9:30–10:00							
10:00–10:30							
10:30–11:00							
11:00–11:30							

Figure 2
Postretirement Weekly Planner

	SUN	MON	TUE	WED	THU	FRI	SAT
6:00–6:30 A.M.							
6:30–7:00							
7:00–7:30							
7:30–8:00							
8:00–8:30							
8:30–9:00							
9:00–9:30							
9:30–10:00							
10:00–10:30							
10:30–11:00							
11:00–11:30							
11:30–Noon							
Noon–12:30 P.M.							
12:30–1:00							
1:00–1:30							
1:30–2:00							
2:00–2:30							
2:30–3:00							
3:00–3:30							
3:30–4:00							
4:00–4:30							
4:30–5:00							
5:00–5:30							
5:30–6:00							
6:00–6:30							
6:30–7:00							
7:00–7:30							
7:30–8:00							
8:00–8:30							
8:30–9:00							
9:00–9:30							
9:30–10:00							
10:00–10:30							
10:30–11:00							
11:00–11:30							

While there are a number of factors contributing to a successful retirement, such as relationships with family and friends, health, living conditions, feelings and attitudes about retirement and aging, and finances, what retired people intend to do with their time is one of the most important ingredients. How will they fill up the extra eight to ten hours, each day, every day, for the rest of their lives, with quality activity?

For most people, work occupies a central place in their lives for many years. They often spend more than eight hours a day at work and in related activities such as driving to and from work, overtime, work brought home, business travel, extra meetings, important projects, and even work-related social functions. There is usually a steady flow of achievement and satisfaction from all this activity, as well as the occasional frustrations and dissatisfactions. Many of us are often unaware of this flow—what I call *mental nourishment*—in our daily work lives because we are conditioned to it over the years. We do, however, become painfully aware of how much the flow means to us when retirement stops our primary source of nourishment altogether.

People often go through their workday hardly aware of the subtle rewards they thrive on: the pride they feel and their various accomplishments. Doing a good job, completing a project, getting a raise or a promotion, helping someone understand a difficult procedure, giving a presentation, or solving a problem are examples of activities that can provide emotional highs. By contrast, for many, retirement doesn't usually provide a flow of accomplishments and satisfactions; there isn't a regular or predictable level of activity that supplies those "sparks" of achievement. The small emotional gratifications of a regular workday are gone. The pressures people had when working, such as maintaining schedules, following plans, meeting deadlines and objectives, commitments, and managing the many other forces that determine their velocity during the day are also removed. Even the anticipation of a Friday or a long weekend is absent. Retirement can bring an open-endedness devoid of the normal cycles to which people have grown accustomed. Adding to these problems is the fact that people's careers were largely instrumental in directing their mode of existence. How they made their living determined what time they got up in the morning, when they ate their meals, and what time they went to bed. Even their periods of leisure were part of a fixed routine and centered about the job. Retirement takes away the discipline that regulates their daily life and even identity.

In retirement, unless people push themselves, they don't go; they have little momentum. They begin to understand that the everyday pressures of working were perhaps an energizing force. A significant number of people have to adjust and learn to function without them. A major source of personal vitality has been severed and something needs to be done before a decline into listlessness and apathy begins. The stimulators that were once a vital if subliminal part of life need to be replaced.

Mike retired after being affiliated for twenty-seven years with a national consumer products company located in the Midwest. As director of training for the company, Mike had the opportunity to be directly responsible for the education and development of many employees who had begun as trainees and successfully progressed over time to vital key positions within the organization. What Mike had done for the company was important and he was often recognized for his contributions, not only by his superiors but also by those employees whom he had trained and for whom he had been an ombudsman. When Mike decided to retire at age fifty-nine, he wasn't prepared for the feelings of loss. He expressed his emotions to me in a questionnaire I had sent him:

> During my career I endured that life with the real satisfaction of doing work that was significant. Retiring and losing that sense of purpose has been deadly for me. I cannot believe how shortsighted and unaware I was when planning for retirement because it never occurred to me how I would respond to being separated from those important day-to-day feelings I was so used to. This realization has had such an impact on me, that I have been almost unable to function for months. I have now begun to consider working again at something with a significant outcome, for pay or as a volunteer, or a combination.

At this point some retirees feel a loss of identity and ask themselves "Who am I now?" It is a feeling of self-diminishment because there has been no foundation for thinking of themselves as functioning outside their career environment. With no basis for understanding what retirement is like, the apprehension of leaving the supportive social, psychological, and intellectual career world provokes speculation and fantasy. After years of being imbedded in a professional and business culture, these people experience difficulty visualizing themselves as retired. This is particularly true for those who are traditionally considered workaholics and for whom work has become all-consuming.

Dennis took early retirement from his job as human resources manager of a large electronics manufacturing company in New York City. Even though he has been able to do some consulting work and teaches an industrial relations course at a local college, an intense sense of displacement is still within him. "I love what I used to do and I just wasn't prepared for functioning away from what I have done for so many years. There are times when I feel like I'm not worth anything anymore."

Surveys by the American Association of Retired Persons (AARP) found that from a quarter to a half of older workers and retirees would delay retirement if they could work fewer hours. In fact, the organization also discovered that 33 percent of its members would still like to be working.

On April 22, 1990, a *New York Times* article titled, "A Move Against Troubling Retirement Leisure," quoted Joseph F. Quinn, an economics professor at Boston College: "It's clear that it doesn't make sense to set up a system where people go from working all the time to working not at all. And yet that's how the workplace has been structured. One week you're working forty hours and the next week you retire and you have no work." Another quote by a woman from the same article says: "When you're working, you get up, you get dressed, you meet new people. I have friends who are just home all the time and it seems that they've gotten into a rut and don't know how to get out."

The end of a career can come very quickly and unexpectedly. Today there are thousands of workers at all organizational levels in their fifties and early sixties caught in the downsizing by companies that are confronted with takeovers, reduced profits, and stronger competition. These people are forced to take severance packages, or have to choose between early retirement and questionable corporate futures. Very often they are not prepared to end their careers and stop working, either psychologically or financially. A March 24, 1989, *Wall Street Journal* article titled, "Early Retirees Fall into Career Oblivion," states: "Because their departures usually are sudden, they have barely contemplated, let alone planned for, what may amount to half their adult life. Instead of relaxation or renewal, retirement has brought anguish and anger."

Surveys from the late 1980s show that a third of retired senior executives return to a full-time job within eighteen months of retirement. The primary reasons for returning are: 1) job satisfaction, enjoyment, or a sense of accomplishment, and 2) a desire to remain active or to avoid boredom. The implication now is that as many retired executives would still like to go back to work, but there are fewer available jobs.

Henry Kates, a former chief executive officer of the Mutual Benefit Life Insurance Company, believes that for some entrepreneurial executives, particularly those who have built up a business or even a division within a larger corporation, the end of a career is tantamount to death; in fact, Kates watched six of his senior managers die soon after retiring. While at Mutual Benefit Kates developed a program to rehire some retired executives who didn't want to give up working but, due to age, had become the victims of a mandatory retirement policy. His new program created special transitional positions for these executives to help ease their move toward eventual retirement. This provided something meaningful for them to do while allowing them the time to explore the possibilities of other employment or get used to the idea of full retirement.

Although few companies have yet gone to the lengths of Mutual Benefit Life Insurance Company, some corporations are beginning to recognize that retirement can be, for some, a traumatic time to which the company may need to help their employees adjust. IBM, for example, provides funding in the amount of $5,000 per retiree for educational or training programs designed to help prepare retirees for either alternative careers or meaningful postretirement activities.

Some retirees are healthy and financially secure enough to do whatever they want, whenever they want; yet they're miserable. Brenda, who retired after twenty-eight years in the apparel industry, thought that being home enjoying the grandchildren and smelling the roses was long overdue. "It was one of the most traumatic things that has ever happened to me. I had this terrible feeling that I had lost my identity. It was a terrible experience for me to attend a cocktail party recently where someone asked, 'What are you doing?' and have to say, 'I'm not doing anything.' "

Sometimes, to compensate for the unease and to fill the retirement void, there is an initial flurry of activity poorly conceived without a clear objective or purpose. The need for some type of preoccupation is compulsive but rarely is it productive. Such activity gives people temporary relief, direction, and purpose, though it lacks depth. The effort to find diversion becomes an example of the bromide, "Keep busy in retirement, that's the key." In reality, for some, their world has turned upside down and is disjointed.

A retired businessman from Tennessee who attended one of my recent seminars told me: "Too much of a good thing became oppressive for me, like golfing or loafing. In my first year in retirement, I took a few cruises; got fed up with that; then went to Las Vegas, and got fed up with that. I played golf in the morning and then a little tennis and still had time to be bored. I started to work part-time and do volunteer work but nothing was satisfying. I started a business which really failed and here I am in your program trying to understand how I can manage my life."

Without proper planning, retirement can be troubling and worrisome. Often, people in retirement do in six months everything that they had been planning for the past thirty years. After that, research shows that many retirees spend their time in the same kinds of activities that occupy employed persons when they are not working. Retirees just spend more time doing these things—a lot more. Research shows that one of the most frequent discretionary activities for many retired persons, believe it or not, is watching television. When work no longer takes up time, people generally reinvest their time in other activities that had previously engaged them and retirees are no different. Based on the fact that retired people typically engage in the same kinds of nonwork activities as do those who are not retired, we can understand why television is such a big part of retirees' lives. *American Demographics* magazine published a survey in 1993 from a Leisure Trends compilation of Americans' use of leisure time. Six thousand Americans were asked in the survey to explain what they do with time they consider their own—their discretionary time. Not included were activities they felt obligated to perform, such as work, commuting, cooking, household chores, child care, food shopping, and the like. While the results of the survey indicated a variety of daily activities, every day was television day and the percentage of time spent each day watching television was significantly higher than the next highest rated activity. For example,

Monday through Thursday, television occupied an average of 33 percent, or five and a quarter hours, of each working day. This figure was somewhat lower for Friday, Saturday, and Sunday: 27 percent, or four and a half hours daily. That seems to be a lot of time spent watching television for those who are not even retired.

One of the many interesting findings in a retirement research project I completed for the New York State Council of School Superintendents in 1991 with 510 retired public school administrators, was what they do with the extra hours of leisure that retirement affords them. The most frequent nonessential activity for these education executives, retired and not working at another job, was watching television. The percentage of time in a typical week or month in this pursuit ranged from a low of 5 percent for some to a high of 75 percent, with the average being almost 48 percent! The other discretionary activities that these retired superintendents engaged in may be of interest and are listed in order of frequency:

- Golf and/or tennis
- Reading
- Volunteering, community work
- Time spent with children/grandchildren
- Travel
- Exercise
- Hobbies
- Gardening
- Church activity
- Household repairs
- Participatory sports
- Fishing
- Socializing
- Caregiving
- Being bored
- Reflecting
- Theater
- Wasting time

Another project involving twelve hundred retired Americans nationwide showed watching television to be a major discretionary activity. The problem is that television for many retirees becomes a way of life, a substitute for other activities that could have more emotional value and return. Television destroys conversation because people rarely talk when it is on. Those who watch a considerable amount of television alone are like solitary drinkers; the set is their entire social life. Television helps reduce thinking and real listening, and destroys dinners together. It's difficult to visit or call friends during prime time.

George Weimer, the executive editor of *Industry Week* magazine calls television the biggest drug in America. "We have become the leading couch potato country," he wrote in the August 3, 1992, issue. "We need to discipline ourselves about this little electric box. We need to turn it off now and then. We need to listen to other people now and then. We need to spend some time with other people and other pursuits. What a boon to us all if we could wean ourselves away from the electronic fix we so dearly need these days."

A major reason for the boredom accompanying retirement is that when many people have been in a focused structure for years, working in one occupation or industry, or several similar ones, for long periods of time, they lose their "peripheral vision." When exposed to a narrow focus, a person's alternatives become restricted. In other words, individuals who have been in one career for most of their lives often have trouble visualizing themselves in another activity or career, especially those professionals who have honed a specific skill for a long period of time.

When people attempt to think about engaging in meaningful activities during this new phase of life, many are unable to develop creative alternatives beyond the usual hobbies and leisure activities, all of which are roles similar to those at work. These retirees take the path of least resistance because they know no other course. Many did not know about the processes of self-assessment, occupational exploration, marketing strategies, and goal-setting (to be discussed in a later chapter).

"Enough money" is the most common answer to the "What do you need for a good retirement?" question. The fact that enough money isn't really enough was made clear to me by a couple I met while traveling recently. As we were all stranded together for several hours in an airport late at night we had ample time to talk. When they learned that I was involved in retirement planning, they naturally began to tell me about their own experiences as a newly retired couple. Since they both appeared to be only in their middle to late forties, I was surprised to learn that they were already retired and had been for two years. With the husband's pension and the money they had made selling a large home in the East, they had enough money to live comfortably in the Sunbelt state they had chosen. They had no children to provide for and no elderly parents or relatives to concern them. At first it sounded too good to be true but, as they talked on, I discovered that despite what appeared to be ideal financial circumstances, they were both restless and dissatisfied.

The first year had been perfect. Everything was new: new home and furnishings completely paid for, new area of the country to explore, new lifestyle to try out, and new people to meet. Everything seemed exciting and fun! It was like a great vacation that goes on and on. What could be better than this? But as the newness of everything around them wore off and the constant whirl of sightseeing, traveling and settling in began to slow, they both realized that they couldn't continue this pace forever. They missed some of the stability and predictable routines they had shed with their jobs and their old lives. As time went on, they tried to keep the same excitement but found it increasingly less satisfying. It was at this point in time that I met them, and they were both considering returning to work or getting counseling. All the free time possible and the money to enjoy it were proving to be less fulfilling than they had always sounded. After working long hours for twenty some years and able to retire quite young, they had no idea of what to do next. Without a plan or goals they were drifting through their days, growing uneasy about the future and their relationship. How much hiking or golf or traveling can anyone really do?

People need to begin the process of discovery again.

Here is an important question: How is it possible to live a meaningful and fulfilled life if work is no longer the center of it? After a few months in retirement, the thrill of sleeping late wears off. Success-motivated people spend most of their adult lives sharpening their abilities, increasing activity, and gaining momentum in their professions. So, in retirement, there is a silent despair for some: they feel irrelevant and think in terms of how much time is left rather than how much time has passed. For them it is the shock of aging.

People in their late fifties and sixties confront the fact as never before: there is a limit to how long we live. This often prevents them from seriously looking at a new career or a major project in terms of whether it can reasonably be completed at this point in life, or even whether they want to spend their remaining years working on it. Some people begin to perceive themselves as much older than their chronological age. Now scanning the obituary page regularly, they see men and women their own age dying with some regularity, and know of others afflicted with progressive disabilities. "I attend more funerals these days than christenings," they say. The result is that some folks begin to personalize death, to see it as something that can happen to them because it's happening to friends. When people feel that time is short and life is drawing to a close, they can lose the motivation necessary for new beginnings. A fresh start at a new career or hobby or even a new friendship may seem futile if one adopts an attitude of "any time now." Resignation and complacency can turn into despair and isolation even when there is no physical reason for this lack of energy and pessimistic outlook. Nothing is more effective as a self-fulfilling prophecy than thinking of oneself as old, tired, and useless. The more time spent in regret and self-pity, the less time is available for getting out in the world and seeking new challenges. The longer this pattern continues the more embedded people may become in a nonfunctional, dead-end lifestyle. So, their behavior begins to change; such people begin to act "old." That can truly be the beginning of the end.

I sometimes remember an older friend who, if he hadn't bought into the aging stereotype, might still be alive today. "I'm growing old," he would say, and blame the aches, pains, and decreased mobility on age. It wasn't his age. It was his feelings and attitudes about becoming older. It was his behavior.

Birthdays influence behavior, causing a reversal in the direction of time as people pass fifty and continue on. It's like the entry into the last part of life. "You count how many birthdays remain instead of how many you have reached." Reaching fifty has a symbolic meaning because it marks half a century, of being at the midpoint. The result is many people become more introspective and take stock of their life. Well, whether fifty, sixty, seventy, or older, people need the freedom to be themselves because there's a lot of living left to do!

5

An Exciting Midlife Filled with Challenge and Adventure

"Before retirement, I saw many who went to the limit in their vocation and then retired lost. I also feel very strongly that because one is successful in one career, that person may also be successful in another and perhaps even another. So I retired and became an actor and model at fifty-five years of age. I am getting too old as a model now, so I just completed a course in voiceovers, where a mature voice is an asset, whereas a mature face is not in demand. I know I have been beaten many times, but I have never accepted defeat."

"I have always felt that retirement is like the night before Christmas; more in anticipation than fulfillment. It has been forever this. Leaving full-time work has been like getting a divorce."

So, you are about to retire—then what? Are you going to be the person who finds everything boring, or the one who can hardly get to sleep at night because you have so many exciting things to do the next day? Imagine your life as a retiree. Think about what an average day or week would be like for you and how you really want the rest of your life to go. Completing the following questionnaire will begin the process and help you focus on some of the important issues discussed in this chapter.

Reader Questionnaire

Suppose you are about to retire:

1. What would you plan to do in retirement?

_____

_____

_____

_____

_____

2. What challenges would you like to attempt?

_____

_____

_____

_____

_____

3. What adventures would you like to pursue?

_____

_____

_____

_____

_____

4. What aspects of your work and work settings will you *miss the most* when you retire?

_____

_____

_____

_____

_____

Retirement is another opportunity to make vital and objective choices about the future. A new career and other long-term targets have their own rewards, while the rocking chair holds no allure. Significant numbers of retirees find no particular dividing line between their pre- and postretirement years; they just find another passion. There are people today who leave one career at retirement and then begin working in a similar vocation or an entirely new one. Of course, some retirees will need to continue working due to financial necessity.

We need to pursue something that keeps us physically, intellectually, and emotionally vibrant. For some, work or a related activity is a tonic, an elixir. Ideally, when people retire, they should have an idea of how they will live and work in the last decades of their lives. Suppose we had been given five years to investigate and work up the kind of activity or goal we would want to be involved in at retirement. In those years, could we develop some ideas, set a course of action, collect information and learn, so that this new direction would be waiting? Couldn't a personal retirement strategy be developed ahead of time?

Unfortunately, with the exception of making financial arrangements, most of us fail to plan for retirement, or are so resistant to the idea that we wait until it confronts us. After the initial few months of retirement novelty wears off, those people who have been professionals and decision makers, now have their spouses telling them to go paint the living room and change all the light bulbs; they just can't tolerate the boredom anymore. Many have never before had to deal with the question, "What will I do today?"

"Just lie on the beach all day and soak up the sun"; "Out on the links all day, every day a golfer's dream"; "Swim, read, hike the nature trails—peace and quiet." These were familiar phrases at cocktail parties in recent years as people discussed their retirement fantasies. After all, retirement was still years away and they could contemplate the details later. Well, "later" came about eighteen months ago for many of them, and for the first six months or so I thought each had indeed achieved their dream.

Pete played golf every day, morning till night, and talked of nothing else: the way his game was improving, the amount of walking he was doing in eighteen holes, the people he met at the club, all interested him and he bubbled over with delight at his new-found freedom. No pressure, no schedule, just golf. Heaven, or so he said then.

Pete called yesterday. It's been a while since we talked and I was curious to hear how he was doing. The answer didn't really surprise me. Pete is bored, tired of the endless golf game which in his busier, preretirement schedule had been a much anticipated and infrequent treat. He had never really had any other outside interests but golf because he was too busy managing his own small business and raising his family, and that was his entire world. Pete has too much free time now for golf to be able to satisfy him the way it once did. The years stretch ahead looking depressingly the same and he needs a change. We talked for a while about what Pete could do to improve the quality of his retirement—a conversation he should have had *long before* he retired. Maybe then he wouldn't have tried to make golf his whole life and he'd be out on the links enjoying the game only occasionally.

In making plans to retire, people should experiment with different activities just as younger folks do when seeking a job after graduation. Connecting with people whose skills or talents you admire can be accomplished by making contacts at career seminars or by joining professional organizations. Volunteering for a few weeks or months in diverse areas is inexpensive and risk-free, and permits you to explore various interests before singling out a particular one. A smorgasbord of choices awaits; there is something for everyone who is willing to seriously begin the process of investigating the unlimited opportunities available.

CONSULTING AND FREELANCING

You can apply your expertise as a consultant in a particular industry after leaving your existing job. Years of contacts in a particular field may make you a prime candidate for consulting firms that service that industry. Being an independent consultant and renting out your experience can be rewarding and exciting, and often you can even select your own working hours.

Companies are hiring freelancers, subcontractors, and independent professionals and many retirees are part of this group. Spurred by global competition, rapid technological change, and narrow profits, companies continue to squeeze out inefficiencies. Whenever possible, corporations are reducing fixed labor costs by contracting out work that consultants can accomplish less expensively or that telecommuters are eager to do from their homes.

Some retirees return to work with the same company as consultants on retainer fee or on an hourly, daily, or project-pay basis. The growing number of early retirees is the result of the corporate obsession with downsizing. Early retirement plans often make organizations leaner but with fewer experienced employees. To compensate for this, companies will gladly engage retirees to fill the void because they don't have to be trained or challenged. In addition, there are few hiring surprises because the person is a known commodity and will be successful performing the job.

David left his position as marketing director with an entertainment company at age fifty-five under an early retirement package. He was promptly hired back with the same company as a consultant three days a week because there was still work that needed to be done. The advantage to the company was extensive: it doesn't have to provide such benefits as medical and life insurance, matching thrift plan and pension contributions, vacation pay or sick days, matching Social Security taxes, and a variety of other costs. The consultant who is not full time keeps expenditures down, doesn't officially increase the head count and doesn't incur for the company the typical administrative expense of having that person in the system.

There are positive incentives for David as well. No taxes are deducted from his fees, and although he is responsible for the tax on the income, he can deduct any bona fide business expenses. By not working full time, he has an opportunity to save more money to fund his retirement as well as to begin the transition to eventual full-time retirement without working. This is similar to the phased-in type of retirement that some companies provide. The consulting arrangement also gives David time to pursue some personal objectives he has established. And it has little of the pressure he typically experienced as a full-time, regular employee because David had seniority, considerable accountability, and a demanding boss.

A friend of mine, Barbara, elected retirement at age sixty from a large national insurance company. She said she had a feeling the company was encouraging her to leave because, though no one said so directly, she was getting too old and too expensive. Two weeks after her retirement dinner at the company, Barbara had her own letterhead and business cards and declared herself a consultant. Barbara had gathered a list of all the small, growing insurance companies in a multistate area around her. Knowing the inherent problems these companies would probably have, she created a marketing letter addressed to the executive officer at each and followed up with a phone call. After two years, she has a number of fledgling companies as clients, offering advice and solutions to their specific problems. "It was hard work in the beginning to get established, but I anticipated that. I'm basically a risk taker with lots of self-motivation. I'm having a lot of fun; it's an entirely new way of life. I can work as hard and as many hours as I want, and take a holiday or vacation when I choose. It's a wonderful balance between doing what I'm very good at doing and still having time for other personal interests."

While it's true that consultants earn impressive fees—$1,150 was the average daily billing in 1993—only one in three make a living at it. But remember, many retirees don't need full-time work and consulting can fit into their lives very conveniently. We are dealing with people who perhaps have had successful careers and have stabilized their lives. Their children are usually out of school, their house is paid for, and they may have some sort of pension arrangement already in place. As a result, they can now say to themselves, "This is what I would like to be involved with for a period of time. I have been through the learning stage, the earning stage, and now I want to go through the living stage!"

VOLUNTEER WORK

Consulting on a volunteer basis can bring just as much recognition of one's talents as any paying job. Retirees may volunteer to work for organizations that need help completing scientific, ecological, social service, and other projects that can't be handled by regular staff because of personnel and financial problems. These projects can be near home or in a foreign land and some of these are discussed in chapter 11. Distance matters less than the deep satisfaction that can be gained from doing worthwhile work of a type you normally don't have an opportunity to do.

Volunteer work is a luxury for most working women. What used to be a mainstay of many organizations, the stay-at-home mom, is a vanishing species. So, at retirement many women find that they have the time and energy to give of themselves and can enjoy many of the traditional types of volunteer jobs that so desperately want and need adult volunteers. Hospitals, hot lines, day care centers, food pantries, and other outlets are just some of the avenues to explore if one wants to volunteer.

One woman I counseled a few years ago had a rather unique

volunteer job. She is a New York State licensed wildlife rehabilitator—a fancy title for one who takes care of orphaned or injured wildlife. While working at a nature center when her children were finally all in school, Mary was asked if she would be interested in helping out at home by caring for two baby raccoons that had been dropped off at the center that morning. They needed round-the-clock care, including bottle feeding, grooming, and medical attention for some skin lesions. Well, these tiny babies were irresistible so of course she agreed, only to be told that she would have to apply for a license and take an oral test given by the Department of Environmental Conservation. It sounded very official and a little frightening, but Mary was committed. She received special permission from the state to care for the orphaned raccoons while awaiting her test date. Several weeks later, as her charges grew fat and healthy, Mary met with a Department of Environmental Conservation representative and passed the test with flying colors. As animals had always been part of her life she already had a lot of the necessary background information but she felt she needed some practical, specific tips and more detailed profiles of each species she was likely to receive. Thus began a search for and involvement in a series of very informative and enjoyable conferences. Mary soon discovered she was part of a large, dedicated group of people who shared her love of animals and desire to be of service. Not only did the conferences provide her with considerable information and new techniques, but they opened up a whole new world of people and programs she never knew existed. Mary told me that her wildlife rehabilitation has been one of the most rewarding experiences of her life. She is able to give back some measure of the joy nature has always given her while performing a much needed and appreciated public service. Such volunteer work is a perfect arrangement for all and especially for retirees who may have the time to give.

Steven's friends and coworkers can't believe his stamina at age sixty-six and assume he quietly collapses every night when he gets home. Steven is employed as a contracts administrator for a small electronics firm that produces sensitive air speed instruments for jet fighter aircraft for the air force and the navy. After work at 5 P.M. Steven drives forty-five minutes to an indoor high school pool, has a yogurt and an apple for his dinner, and by 6:30 P.M. he is in his bathing suit greeting the evening students who are participating in his lifeguard training course. Steven is a volunteer for the American Red Cross and a certified water safety instructor who teaches a variety of aquatic programs year round four days a week. Steven's lifeguard course lasts from 7 until 9:30 in the evening, and by the time he has given individual help at the end of each class to those who ask, swum his quarter mile (eighteen laps in the pool), showered, and driven home, it's 11:30 P.M. Saturdays and Sundays Steven volunteers as an emergency medical technician with the local ambulance corps.

"How do you do it?" I asked.

Well, I'm single so family obligations don't interfere with my schedule. After leaving my weekly job each evening and diving into that pool and doing a few laps, I feel refreshed and ready for teaching class. I have always been a good swimmer and used to lifeguard in the 1940s, so ten years ago I took a course and was recertified. Then I took and passed a water safety instructor course, which qualified me to teach a wide range of programs. I get a great sense of pride and accomplishment seeing all those people of different ages graduate and receive their certificates. When I retire, I'll just have more time to volunteer and I'm looking forward to it. This kind of volunteering keeps me feeling young by association and keeps me in shape. Heck, I'm in better shape than many of the teenagers who take my course.

Sometimes volunteer work benefits the helper as much as the organization or people being helped. In his book *The Healing Power of Doing Good* Allan Luks compares the feeling of euphoria that many volunteers experience when helping to the endorphin-induced buzz of "runner's high." He claims that "helper's high," as he calls it, relieves stress and raises self-esteem. This can be important for retirees and, of course, volunteering helps individuals connect with one another—people from different backgrounds having fun together, reaching out to each other. If you would like to become involved in volunteering, need some ideas, and want to find a volunteer group in your area, call or write to: The Points of Light Foundation, 1737 H Street NW, Washington, D.C. 20006, (800) 879-5400.

TEMPORARY JOBS

Older workers are back in demand and this trend will continue to grow. The nonworking population of our country is growing faster than the working segment, and soon the country could be seriously short of skilled people. Some organizations are starting to capitalize on older workers by providing part-time employment, and opportunities are expanding in temporary jobs. These jobs provide the satisfaction of work and still allow for whatever else older workers want to do with their lives.

Days Inn, for example, continues to encourage its hotels to hire older workers through a "Senior Power Jobs Fair" program. In the late 1980s, the hotel's average employee turnover rate was 180 percent, with a 30 percent absentee rate. So Days Inn began to attract workers from the over fifty-five labor market. So committed was the company that it even began putting up notices at senior centers to hire older workers nationwide as managers, reservation agents, desk clerks, group sales agents, and bellhops. The absentee rate is down to about 3 percent and the average tenure is over three years for the older employees.

At the annual "Ability Is Ageless" job fair sponsored by the New York City Department for the Aging's senior employment division, fifty employers attended the December 1993 fair to market their companies and attract older job candidates. Major firms representing such industries as banking, accounting, insurance, jewelry, entertainment, food service, and communications offered a variety of management, sales, and administrative positions to qualified seniors.

A recent interview with the National Association of Temporary Services in Alexandria, Virginia, a professional organization of over one thousand member companies in the United States that supply labor on a temporary basis, revealed that in 1993, 11 percent of the workers were retired people. Considering there are about 1,640,000 people working on a temporary basis each day, that translates into 180,400 retirees, a sizeable number. The organization also said that many of its member firms have separate divisions for retired people, and there are some companies that specialize in retirees. Another interesting comment was that there has been an increase in the volume of requests for temporary workers with specific advanced skills, for example, engineering, senior management, and scientific. The older market tends to be better qualified. In many cases it is only the retirees who have the skills because they are the only ones both qualified and available.

Eldertemps is an employment service located in Potomac, Maryland, that deals exclusively with workers fifty years of age and over. The firm primarily handles administrative and general office support personnel and some professionals for both temporary assignments as well as permanent positions. In a March 1994 telephone discussion, President Roberta (Rob) Walker said that her organization receives requests from companies and professional and trade associations that are looking for productive and qualified workers regardless of their age, with some preferring the older employee. "Qualified people are decreasing in the younger worker pool and the younger candidate often doesn't have the business deportment and breadth of experience that an older worker does," Walker said.

Small businesses are taking a serious look at the growing reservoir of skilled men and women in their fifties, sixties, and even seventies who are valuable economic resources. Most possess proven skills and maturity of judgment. They tend to be very reliable performers whose attendance record is usually better than that of their younger colleagues. Older employees display more company loyalty than youthful workers, resulting in lower turnover. Creative and intellectual achievements don't decline with age and the work ethic is often stronger in the older person. A new company may discover that the senior hiree is able to make quick contributions in a variety of areas such as sales, marketing, manufacturing, and management. Because of his or her other experience the older employee will be more objective, conservative, perhaps have a more positive temperament under pressure, and offer sound alternatives when a key decision is under consideration. This is an important advantage for the smaller company that cannot afford financial mistakes. The senior employee is often an excellent mentor and role model for the younger staff members who do not feel threatened by this person.

According to the Bureau of Labor Statistics, most of the new jobs the economy will create over the next decade will be in the service sector. Banking, health care, food service, transportation, counseling, interviewing, real estate, hotels, travel agencies, market research, retail, and leisure and recreation require face-to-face contact. Since there will be dramatic increases of older people in America, customers are most comfortable dealing with someone like themselves. This process of age matching is very effective. Also, many new jobs will require higher levels of mathematics, language, and reasoning ability than in the past, knowledge and skills that older workers possess in abundance. Older workers have a certain ability to deal with problems, a certain decision-making ability and, above all in the service industry, an ability to deal with people.

RETURNING TO SCHOOL

Many retiring people want to continue their education. Perhaps retirement offers the first opportunity for them to return to school and learn something that has nothing directly to do with their work. They can acquire new skills and knowledge just because the subject excites and stimulates them, and may have a meaningful impact on their lives. The learning environment is also one of the best ways to meet new friends. Few realize that when they retire, as many as 90 percent of their previous relationships with people will be severed. Older adults can enroll in many full-time programs, or attend as few as one or two classes a week, or even take a learning vacation on a college campus.

By 1998, college students twenty-five years of age and older across the country will be the majority on campuses, reports a study by the College Board and the U.S. Department of Education. Because of decreasing enrollments, many colleges have been forced to lure adult students in order to survive, offering them a variety of incentives from substantial tuition discounts or no tuition and life-experience credits among others. Returning to school is attractive to many adults, though it usually has little to do with degree studies; it simply stimulates them. Other mature learners are returning to community colleges, universities, and vocational schools to receive degrees for the first, second, or third time or else to prepare for career changes. Many colleges offer adult options where older students register for courses at a minimal fee or without charge. These students don't turn in assignments or participate in class and do not take course examinations, but they can observe and learn. Since finances can be a concern, where special arrangements are not available or for those who want to pursue the traditional program of study, financial aid is made available to qualified older students.

Some adults wishing to return to school are concerned with their ability to be able to do the work required when taking courses for credit. "At my age I'm unsure of my ability to remember information, to concentrate, to have the physical and mental energy to succeed, and whether I can capture those study skills I had forty years ago," one hesitant sixty-year-old woman told me. Does this sound like the geronotophobia described in chapter 3? Research shows that it isn't age that establishes a person's mental ability, but the amount of mental stimulation. In a survey of faculty members conducted by the Gerontology Center at Wichita State University in Kansas to measure the behavior of older adults in the classroom, more than 75 percent of respondents said older students were at least as quick to learn as younger ones. Sixty-four percent said they seemed more motivated, and three out of five faculty members responded that older students made a positive difference in their classes.

At the University of Memphis, Tennessee, older students are not only encouraged in their desire to return to school, they are eased through the transition by the MINI (Move Into a New Identity) College program. This program is designed specifically for older adults who may not have been on a college campus for twenty years or more, and helps them through the types of adjustments older students face. While many have to relearn some study skills, older students end up being some of the finest on campus.

Let me relate two unusual examples: Eli Finn returned to study, at the age of one hundred, at Springfield College three days each week and enrolled in two U.S. foreign relations courses. He isn't distracted by short-skirted coeds, climbing four flights of stairs, or the drive to school. Daniel Wynkoop, eighty-six years old, finally received his Yale University degree a few years ago, sixty-five years after he was expelled from Yale for getting married.

ENTREPRENEURSHIP

Entrepreneurship is another alternative many in retirement choose to pursue. Men and women who are considering retirement or who have recently retired are particularly inclined to break the old patterns, leave routine jobs behind, and make a fresh start. From a personal standpoint, retirement could be a good time for people to go into business for themselves, perhaps turning a favorite hobby into a thriving enterprise. They have more time to devote to a career, a good idea of what they would like to do, and perhaps the experience necessary to see it through. The Small Business Administration estimates that as many as 20 percent of the over one million business startups each year are initiated by men and women fifty or over. Not only can a small business for fun and profit generate a feeling of accomplishment, but it also can supplement a retirement income. Typically, a good business idea translates into a product or service that appeals to buyers and matches the retiree's skills and interests. More and more people are discovering that the conventional work years can be the prelude to new worlds of opportunity.

After retirement at age sixty-five, Mary Holzer, who always loved painting, started painting scenes of Native American life. She thought they would make interesting greeting cards so she had five designs printed at a cost of $250 for several dozen cards. The cards have proven so popular that Mary's designs are now ordered by three of the major greeting card companies, particularly for the holiday seasons. She also markets her cards independently to specialty and hotel gift shops and works out of her home, where she employs a small staff, including her husband.

Mario had been a barber at a country club for thirty-five years when he retired to take a seasonal, part-time job as a gardener for a former customer who owned a large estate. When Mario, who loves music, learned how much the family paid regularly to have its two pianos tuned, he investigated how to become a piano tuner. After taking a correspondence course recommended by the Piano Technicians Guild in Kansas City and then spending time as an apprentice with an experienced piano tuner, Mario advertised and began to market his new business. He now has a cluster of regular customers at colleges, grammar and high schools, vocational schools, churches, fraternal organizations, nursing homes, and private residences. Mario loves it, and his new career gives him the opportunity to meet many people and develop relationships, something that was very important to him when he was a barber.

Valerie had worked as a dietician in a large community hospital for seventeen years and her husband, Bob, was an accountant for the local public utility company. Always concerned about good health and the role nutrition and exercise contributes to a positive lifestyle, they frequently attended lectures at the local colleges on emerging health issues. Determined to continue their interests in retirement, Valerie and Bob decided to open a health food store in a location near their home town. Bob and Valerie knew that the profit margins in health foods and vitamins were high enough to make the average supermarket owner green with envy. They also knew that by starting small in a major market like health food, they could build the business through sharp marketing and promotional skills, knowledge of nutrition, and good business, merchandising, and buying sense. Because their children were grown and their home mortgage almost paid, Valerie and Bob were able easily to obtain a home equity loan to meet the business startup investment cost of around $80,000. Their combined savings from matching 401K plans at work were still secure and within four years they moved their store to larger quarters to meet the demand.

One woman chose to develop and manage a small, exclusive retail store. She carefully planned and researched her objective before she retired, attending two evening courses at a local college in retail sales and management. This enabled her to fully understand and evaluate the implications of a retail business, including the financial and tax aspects. She assessed the space requirements and investigated possible locations for the store—learning about space utilization and leasing in the process. Exploring pricing with wholesale suppliers provided new ideas and answers about merchandise. She educated herself about the pros and cons of incorporation. When her retirement date arrived, she knew exactly what she wanted to do and how to do it. Today, she owns a very successful store and mail-order business, while still having time for leisure activities.

To help people focus on a variety of ideas, *Entrepreneur* magazine publishes an annual "Small Business Development" catalog, which is free (just call 800-421-2300) and lists over 190 full- and part-time business opportunities for America in the 1990s. The catalog outlines these business opportunities in different categories, including business services, home services, leisure, computers, children's food, pets, retail, apparel, and automotive, and provides methods, strategies, and guidelines to manage each. It also lists profit, potential risks, as well as minimum and average startup investment costs. The federal Small Business Administration (SBA) publishes free and inexpensive pamphlets that address the needs of new entrepreneurs. For a free catalog, call your local SBA office, listed in the telephone book under "United States Government Offices" or telephone (800) 827-5722.

There are limitless activities for retired people. I often receive letters from people telling me about the interesting and exciting midlife opportunities they have followed after retirement. One married couple joined an oceanic research expedition in the Bahamas. Others decide to join the Peace Corps, which has no age limit. In return for sharing their expertise they get a chance to travel and an unforgettable living experience in a foreign country, along with expenses and housing.

I know of people who have become hosts and hostesses on cruise lines, volunteered as campground hosts at state and national parks, or worked on research projects around the world in fields like archaeology, anthropology, and animal behavior. One retired couple turned their country home into a bed and breakfast inn.

Retirement is not an end to significant activity but rather a new beginning filled with excitement and adventure. Today, the basic assumption about the linear life plan is rapidly changing. It's no longer the case that most of life's periods of growth take place in the first half of life, while the second half is generally characterized by decline.

What's wrong with having a couple of careers while still having time for travel and planned leisure? People are living longer and longer today. The age range of sixty to seventy is today more like that of forty to fifty a couple of decades ago. Getting older is a fact and people have to be prepared to meet its challenges. Part of the challenge is to plan to add life to all the years ahead. People need to believe that they are standing on the edge of an exciting future, on a threshold —at the beginning of a new adventure. The important thing is for people to decide, while they are still in their careers, what goals they wish to reach while in their chosen profession and thereafter. Deciding what to do isn't always easy as people reach this important juncture in their lives.

In my workshops on retirement and life planning for those not yet retired, I ask the participants what they get out of their work, or I may ask, "When you leave work and retire, what will you miss most about your job?" The replies are wide-ranging: "a sense of belonging"; "a daily structure and routine"; "the interpersonal contacts"; "useful- ness and having a sense of purpose"; "a place to go each day"; "a challenge"; "helping others"; "making money"; "the gossip and keep- ing connected"; "the chance to dress up"; "power, influence, and mak- ing decisions"; "personal achievement"; "recognition"; "socializing"; "having an identity"; "being needed"; "escape from home life";

"anticipation of a long weekend or going on vacation"; "the opportunity to associate with younger people"; "working as a team with others"; "pride in my work"; "learning something new"; "the opportunity to travel"; "being creative"; and "romance and flirting in the workplace."

Then I may ask the participants in the seminar what they will substitute for those things they just identified when they leave their jobs and retire. This usually is followed by a period of silence because many people don't have an answer. They haven't considered how and even if they will replace many of those forces that have been part of their lives for so many years and provided their daily momentum.

People should begin to think about what they are going to do with the rest of their lives. What do they want? Many people have no idea. It is like being shipwrecked. Retirement forces people to ask some questions about their lives that were never asked before: "Do I start all over again?" "Do I have the energy and the motivation or even the interest?" "Does it even matter?"

Some people toil, searching for activities and goals that will give them a mission, a purpose. Some try golf, volunteer work, opening a small business, or travel. "Is there anything that will energize me?" It's like being adrift with no land in sight. A number of people do not fit into the "I do what I want when I want, and if I don't do anything, so what?" category.

There are a variety of approaches to assist a person who is undecided to prepare and begin a course of action. Here are a few:

Earlier we discussed how many people will miss certain things about leaving work that can be called "personal needs," and that some of these needs should be replaced in retirement. Figure 3, "Personal Needs and Replacements for Work," is an interesting exercise that has proven successful in helping many preretirees and retirees begin an objective process to establish meaningful goals and achieve them while retired.

The left column lists some examples of the typical personal needs people feel are important when working. We mentioned some of these earlier in this chapter. To illustrate how to proceed we will begin with an actual situation:

Walter had been in education his entire career at a variety of positions, culminating in public school superintendent; at age fifty-seven he elected to retire. Having been continuously exposed to challenges and solving problems, and being a high achiever with a strong identity, Walter

Figure 3
Personal Needs and Replacements for Work

Needs Met by Your Job	Future Activity to Meet These Needs	Steps to Reach Goal	Timetable	Possible Obstacles	Alternative Strategy or Goal
Interpersonal Contacts; Social Supports		1. 2. 3.		1. 2. 3.	
Compensation		1. 2. 3.		1. 2. 3.	
Structure: Organization of Life		1. 2. 3.		1. 2. 3.	
Usefulness; Having a Sense of Purpose		1. 2. 3.		1. 2. 3.	
Goals		1. 2. 3.		1. 2. 3.	
Challenge		1. 2. 3.		1. 2. 3.	
Sense of Accomplishment; Achievement		1. 2. 3.		1. 2. 3.	
Power and Influence; Making Decisions		1. 2. 3.		1. 2. 3.	
Sense of Belonging		1. 2. 3.		1. 2. 3.	

Figure 3 (cont'd)

Needs Met by Your Job	Future Activity to Meet These Needs	Steps to Reach Goal	Timetable	Possible Obstacles	Alternative Strategy or Goal
Structure for the Day; A Routine		1. 2. 3.		1. 2. 3.	
A Recognizable Identity		1. 2. 3.		1. 2. 3.	
Helping Others		1. 2. 3.		1. 2. 3.	
(To be filled in by reader)		1. 2. 3.		1. 2. 3.	
(To be filled in by reader)		1. 2. 3.		1. 2. 3.	

was apprehensive about the void retirement would create for him. He anticipated difficulty adjusting to the fact that he would no longer be the center of issues, though he would be free of the stress and the related health problems that accompanied his superintendency.

Determined to make his retirement productive and rewarding, Walter focused on "challenge," "sense of accomplishment," "achievement," and "a recognizable identity" as primary needs he wanted in his future activities. These were important to him and it was a challenge imagining retirement without these aspects.

Filling out the form, Walter thought that all three of these needs could be met by his longtime desire to write a book about the education system and how it could be improved. This was not an easy objective and Walter knew there would have to be substantial preparation. The first step in reaching his goal would be to attend two courses at a local college on creative writing and one course titled, "Is There a Book

Inside You?" The second step would be to outline the book and then write at least six of the fourteen chapters he had outlined. The third step was to target some literary agents and send each a proposal along with two sample chapters. The timetable Walter established for the three steps was three months, five months, and one month respectively. In other words, his objective was to have completed, at the end of nine months, the three steps and sent proposals to agents. Walter anticipated about 65 percent of his time would be spent working toward his objective and the rest would be spent in partnership with his wife accomplishing some activities they had planned.

Walter considered a few possible obstacles, which he wrote on the form. One was that the literary agents would reject his proposal or were not considering any new authors. Another was that he wouldn't be able to complete the six chapters in the time frame. His alternate strategies were to try to go directly to selected publishers, rather than through an agent, and, if unsuccessful, to consider self-publishing. Another would be to extend his timetable. His alternate goal, if everything failed, would be to write articles for magazines and professional education journals coupled with speaking engagements.

This is an example of how one individual carefully researched and planned one retirement objective in order to fulfill some of the needs he would have when he left work as an educator.

While we have discussed that total leisure may not be an ideal retirement for everyone, it certainly can be a regular activity that offers a balance in retirement life. Many pre- and postretirees don't have clear ideas about what their true leisure interests are. "What's the matter with going out on the boat and fishing again? You can sit in the boat and read—you said you didn't mind that. Besides, what else is there to do?" a retired husband may say to his wife. Rather than taking this path of least resistance it would help to clarify other leisure alternatives. It is a path to discovery, learning, and being creative, as opposed to overlooking ideas or being bored by and annoyed with uninteresting routines.

The Inventory of Retirement Activities (IRA) published by Crisp Publications is a self-administered pencil and paper exercise designed to help pre- and postretirees develop interests worthy of their leisure time and activities to suit their personalities. It helps make the user aware of options available and prompts objective planning. The exercise is in three parts and takes about thirty minutes to complete. People can discover, for example, that they have interests compatible with those of a partner and friends. It is a fact that some people go through life not knowing many of the interests of people close to them. Capitalizing on similar interests is one way for two people to more fully enjoy retirement. Those who take the IRA will discover other interesting profiles that will help guide the retiree through the maze of planning options. This publication may be ordered from Crisp Publications, Inc., at (800) 442-7477, or by writing to 1200 Hamilton Court, Menlo Park, CA 94025.

Many facing retirement and those already retired would like to become involved in a meaningful activity such as beginning a new career or developing a small business. We discussed in chapter 4 how some people don't have a clue what interesting alternatives are available; those people need a self-assessment process to discover what choices are out there.

One effective appraisal instrument I have used successfully for years is the Self-Directed Search (SDS), published by Psychological Assessment Resources, Inc. The SDS is easily completed, scored, and interpreted by the user. Through a series of questions about aspirations, activities, occupations, skills, and self-estimates, the SDS motivates the pre- or postretiree to evaluate his or her abilities and interests. It increases self-understanding and indicates compatible work or volunteer environments by guiding the user to a variety of careers. The SDS is based on the premise that most people can be categorized into six personality types: Realistic, Investigative, Artistic, Social, Enterprising, or Conventional, and that people search for work environments dominated by those respective characteristics. I have found that the SDS has opened the eyes of many people to career ideas they had not previously considered or even thought possible. After all, some people retire and then embark on as many as two or three different careers over the next fifteen to twenty-five years.

Another useful tool is the Leisure Activities Finder (LAF), which is a guide containing 760 hobbies, sports, and avocations. This can be used in conjunction with the SDS to locate leisure activities that are purposeful and genuinely satisfying. For further information and/ or to order, call Psychological Assessment Resources, Inc., at (800) 331-8378, or write P.O. Box 998, Odessa, FL 33556. Both the LAF and SDS can be purchased for under twenty dollars.

Without a challenge or an opportunity to grow, many older people would cease to have meaning in their lives. One person wrote, "If I had no responsibility or place to go, I would just sit down and die. I'd rust out if I sat down. As long as you keep growing you won't get ripe—as long as you aren't ripe you won't rot and die."

Someone once said that by the time we die we have discovered only 25 percent of our talents and interests. It's an unprovable assertion but one worth believing because the retirement adventure is the ideal time to locate that missing 75 percent!

6

"What Are We Going to Do When We Retire, Dear?"

"A large part of my feelings of relaxation is the fact that my wife retired at the same time as I did and we have faced the challenges together. Our relationship has deepened and been a source of happiness and support, and this is likely a major factor in my overall retirement satisfaction and pleasure."

"It is extremely important to begin retirement planning years ahead and to include your spouse in the process. It has been difficult for us and we almost had to begin our life all over again—it seemed we had grown apart over the years and the immediate togetherness in retirement forced us to reevaluate our relationship. Fortunately things worked out after a few years. It's also very important to develop several similar interests as well as having independent ones. The things we take for granted—we often never realize."

Many couples yearn for more time together during the busy career and child-rearing years of their marriage. It is often assumed that dissatisfactions in the relationship would be lessened if only they had more free time to spend with each other. Retirement can provide extra time but frequently couples find that they have different ideas about how to spend that time; perhaps this can be part of the adventure. The following few questions for you to think about before reading on may help prepare you for some of the considerations.

1. Do you think a satisfactory preretirement relationship with your partner is a good indicator of a satisfactory relationship after you retire?
   Yes ( ) No ( )

2. How would you feel if your spouse should choose to return to work after you had retired?

   _____

   _____

   _____

3. What concerns would you have if you decided to continue working after your partner's retirement?

   _____

   _____

   _____

4. Do you think household chores such as doing the laundry, general housecleaning, and the like, are responsibilities to be shared equally during retirement?
   Yes ( ) No ( )
   If not, how do you see your role?

   _____

   _____

   _____

5. What things do you think may need changing in your relationship with your spouse and how will you deal with those things that will not change?

   _____

   _____

   _____

The husband was astonished. "I paid almost three dollars for this small jar of peanut butter!" His wife had always done the shopping, but since recently retiring he had decided to get the groceries for something to do. The poor fellow nearly went into shock.

While putting the food away another recent retiree found a package of cooking yeast in the pantry. When his wife came home he said, "It's time to use the packet of yeast before it expires at noon tomorrow."

Until such time as today's two-income couples reach retirement, there will be a mistaken tendency to view part of the retirement process as one in which the man is displaced while his wife remains relatively unaffected, except for the annoyance of having him underfoot, the unwelcome attempt to reorganize the household for greater efficiency, and the complaints about the high cost of food. The image held by many is that the wife's life essentially does not change. This reminds us of an adage, which, unfortunately, is often true: "The man retires but the woman never does." The truth of the matter is that a man's retirement strongly affects his wife and has a significant impact on their relationship.

Carol was in bed reading at eleven o'clock on Monday morning when Joey, her husband, came into the bedroom and asked her if she was sick. "No, I feel fine," she replied. "So why are you still in bed?" Joey asked, confused. "I'm retired," replied Carol. "What the hell does that mean?" her husband asked in a sharp tone of voice. "It means I'm retired—just like you, and I'm retired from doing the laundry every day, food shopping every week, cleaning and picking up your clothes, doing the bills and balancing the check book, and cooking. I'm tired of all of it just like you got tired of work!"

Years ago a friend of mine decided to build a house in a remote area of New Hampshire where he and his wife were going to live when they retired. I asked him what he was going to do there for a third of his life. He said, "Hunt, fish, go hiking and canoeing, develop a pine forest, and perhaps build a small hunting lodge near the lake. Don't worry, I'll have enough to keep me busy." I knew his wife had an artistic personality and often pursued her interests in cultural activities; she was not an outdoors person. I asked my friend what his wife was going to do for the rest of her life after they retired and moved to New Hampshire. At first I thought he hadn't understood the question because he looked incredulous, but then I realized this was an issue he had not yet seriously considered. He finally replied, "There will be plenty for her to do just helping me."

Another couple I know recently moved to a Florida retirement community adjacent to a golf course. The husband is delighted; he's in paradise. He loves the sun. He likes the competitive spirit and enjoys golf five days a week. He plays tennis, and has invested in a local driving range. His wife, however, is unhappy. She doesn't enjoy the constant hot weather, doesn't play tennis, and isn't a good golfer. She is disenchanted with the retirement community, because everyone is about the same age, all have similar interests, and they usually discuss the same things. She is sixty-two years old, in good health, and not looking forward to living there for another twenty-five years. Though trying desperately to live up to her husband's expectations, she feels that she is unable to continue with the situation much longer. Frustrated, she doesn't know what to do but does not want to upset her husband's dream.

Consider the working wife who, five years ago, reentered the workforce after twenty-six years to help with the college expenses for her children. She is now fifty-eight and her husband, who just retired at age sixty-five, is unable to understand why she is not ready to retire with him. "I'm not ready to give up my job," she said. "I enjoy the self-esteem along with the intellectual stimulation and social contacts my job brings. Also, I don't know if I could tolerate such constant closeness every day with my husband." Now her husband stays at home alone and refuses to find something productive to do on his own. He is depressed, telephones her at work three to four times each day, and is beginning to drink heavily. When she arrives home after a full work day he asks, "What's for dinner?"

It's tricky to synchronize the timing of the transition for two people, especially if they have independent careers. Often one partner has fixed expectations about retirement, one expectation being that his or her partner will retire at the same time.

It seems to be easier for single people.

At my high school reunion a few years ago I ran into one of my favorite teachers, who was in town and had dropped in to see "her kids." Her "kids," now in their fifties, were curious about what Miss Proulx was doing now, after ten years of retirement, even as they were beginning to consider their own. Was she happy? Was she married? Was she working? Where was she living? Miss Proulx (I still can't call her Marie) cheerfully answered all the questions thrown at her and then sat down with me for a more in-depth look at her rather unusual retirement.

Miss Proulx had never married and had no children or living parents to take care of. She didn't even own a cat. She was literally free as a bird when, at the age of sixty-seven, she decided to bring to a close her long and extremely satisfying career teaching high school English. After thirty-eight years it was time, she felt, for something new. Intrigued by her decidedly upbeat, enthusiastic attitude, I encouraged her to discuss her postcareer life and to share her thoughts about why she had been so successful in planning her retirement, which she was so obviously enjoying.

Miss Proulx's answers were in keeping with my good retirement planning program but were unique because of her being single. As a teacher, she said, she had always traveled extensively around the United States and abroad; this had given her a good idea of the types of climate, lifestyle, and services that she found attractive as well as those she knew were not for her. Naturally, Miss Proulx said, a city or town with a university seemed an obvious choice for a retiring teacher. Whenever she traveled she spent some time at the nearest college or university to check out the library and see what classes, trips, and cultural events were available. The climate was not nearly as important to her as proximity to good transportation: train stations, airports, buses, and subways. Miss Proulx still did not drive after all these years! Her dependence on public transportation narrowed her choices somewhat but she was very resourceful and an experienced traveler. Most large cities in every part of the country as well as overseas have at least adequate bus service or subways or both. Miss Proulx was never very attracted to wilderness or nature, so for her this limitation was not really an issue. As she took her summers off every year, she was able to spend enough time in each city or region that she visited to form a realistic picture of what living there would be like. She always tried to get short-term rental apartments when she traveled, thereby necessitating trips to local grocery stores, laundromats, and the like, and daily use of the bus service. She actually lived in the city or town as opposed to simply visiting it and seeing only a tourist's view. Walking tours were her favorite tourist activity, affording her an intimate look at specific areas.

Because of her single, childless status Miss Proulx did not have to consider anyone else's needs, interests, or attitudes when choosing a retirement lifestyle or location. She traveled alone most of the time but maintained close friendships all across the country that provided plenty of companionship when she needed it. Most of the time she was content to be alone. This freedom from pressure of adjusting to and trying to satisfy another person's idea of what life should be like was, she felt, an important factor in her successful retirement. Miss Proulx pleased only herself.

Equally important, I feel, is her positive attitude and endless curiosity about the world and her fellow human beings. Miss Proulx had always had a focus for her summer vacations: whether studying Spanish missions in California or taking a jazz tour of the South, she was always involved in learning something new. After retiring she continued to plan her trips, and to a certain extent her daily life, around education. A letter to the editor of her local paper complaining about the occasional discrimination she experienced as a solo traveler led to an offer of a job writing a weekly "tips for a single travelers" column. She accepted, of course. An avid reader, Miss Proulx is also involved in a monthly book discussion group and tries to volunteer weekly at the local hospital reading to terminally ill children. Her life is full, busy, and purposeful, and she doesn't even own a television because, as she pointed out, "Whenever would I have the time to watch it?"

Miss Proulx is a good example of how complete and satisfying the next chapter of life can be when approached in a positive way with careful planning and sufficient income. In case you're curious, she currently lives in a condominium in the heart of San Diego, California.

For married couples, the major problem rests with how they approach their retirement. For example:

She: "What are we going to do when we retire, dear?"
He: "Well, I don't know. I haven't given it much thought, but we have plenty of time to think about it."
She: "I guess you're right. I'm sure we will decide on something. After all, a few of our friends who are retired often say that they're busier now than before they retired."

Over the next few years there will be some attention paid to their investments, pensions, and Social Security benefits to determine if their postretirement standard of living can be reasonably similar to their preretirement standards. Suddenly, retirement is a reality and neither one has focused clearly on the actual living of those retirement years. After a while, one or both partners sense that something is wrong at a time when they need things to go smoothly. Sometimes their capacity to communicate, to talk objectively and sincerely, is restrained and honest dialogue becomes difficult. Often problems are resolved without discussion, because one partner acquiesces to the other, perhaps unaware of doing so, and does not consider the future consequences.

Now in her late fifties, Sarah has discovered she's a career person, and she loves it, but her husband Leo is not enchanted. When the subject of retirement surfaces, neither Sarah nor Leo is willing or able to express their worries. "What will we have to talk about? Will we get bored with life and each other? Will we need friends along if we decide to travel just to lessen the intensity we feel when we are alone? What will we do each day with no differentiation between Monday and Saturday—a week-long weekend? Sarah has decided to continue her career indefinitely because she secretly doesn't know how to address these issues. "Right now, it's the easier path to take. Big choices, new stages, and very little history to refer to for help. Our mothers didn't have this problem and there's no course at college offering guidance in this area. Let Leo retire first and get settled in some kind of routine and then I'll see. I just don't want to deal with it now." I can already predict how this will turn out if they don't take a serious look at what retirement means to both of them.

Retirement can open up issues between spouses that had been hidden by child rearing and occupational routines. After a couple has stopped working and the children have left home, often there is little to talk about. Suddenly the relationship you've taken for granted is open to reevaluation. A few years ago, at the conclusion of one of my retirement planning workshops in Chicago, a woman came to me and said: "Your program could have saved our marriage if my husband and I had attended five years ago."

We sat down and I asked her to explain what she meant.

"My ex-husband retired a few years ago after a successful thirty-one-year career as a financial executive" with a major international company, she said. "Our children were grown and no longer lived at home. We began our retirement trying to do everything together, to sort of make up for lost time because we had been so busy working.

"After a while we smothered each other. We began to argue, then drifted apart, and finally divorced. It's an interesting irony that the divorce forced each of us to finally plan our lives, though separately. We each had to ask ourselves, 'What am I going to do with the rest of my life?' We had to decide what to do with the house and other assets, what the financial arrangements would be, and so on.

"The divorce forced us to deal with the questions about future relationships. If we had invested the time discussing and planning our retirement relationship before we retired that we did when we divorced, we probably would still be together. Your program made me realize all the things we didn't do but should have."

Sometimes, many of the hopes and expectations about retirement die before they have an opportunity to become reality. It's unfortunate that some couples who have been "happily married" for many years are unable to make the retirement transition together successfully.

Interesting, isn't it: couples talk endlessly about getting married and living together as partners, and then have heart-to-heart talks about whether to have children and when. Soon the need arises to discuss buying a house, day care, and schools. How is it that couples can comprehend the vital need for careful give and take on these life issues but often neglect to make the same effort with the subject or retirement?

The National Center for Statistics and American Demographics reports that 7.8 percent of married couples will divorce after twenty-five years of marriage, 3.8 percent after thirty years of marriage, 2.0 percent after thirty-five years of marriage, and 1.0 percent after forty years. The National Center for Women and Retirement Research indicates that there are nearly ten thousand divorces each year involving at least one spouse over the age of sixty-five. The AARP even publishes a how-to guide titled *Getting Divorced after Fifty*.

"Who would have ever believed it would turn out like that?" my wife asked as she hung up the telephone. "How did what turn out, and who was that?" I asked. It turned out that she had been talking to the wife of a neighbor of ours from years ago. Janet and Mike had married only ten years before—a second marriage for both. Between them they finished raising their six children and when the last one went to college they thought about retiring. Mike worked for one of the big companies that was restructuring and, because he was then fifty-two, he was offered an early retirement incentive—a deal he couldn't refuse. Both he and Janet thought that lifetime health benefits and a hefty pension were the promise of "happily ever after." But things did not go well after Mike's retirement. Janet had just told my wife that she was leaving Mike. The retirement they had both looked forward to had torn their marriage apart.

What happened was different expectations, rigid behavior, and a shifting focus in the marriage. When Janet and Mike both had jobs and separate lives revolving around their children from previous marriages, time alone together was at a premium. The luxury of lying around a beach (or even a backyard) all day just relaxing was a treat. They looked forward to the rare occasions when all the teenagers were busy and accounted for elsewhere. Vacations tended to be short and were close by and most often a whirlwind of children, pets, and relatives. Peace and quiet was what looked good to them then.

As the children grew and moved away the pace slowed but college, weddings, and grandchildren filled the gap. Life went on as busily as before. Janet stopped working first, as hers had become a part-time position in the last year anyway. She really enjoyed being home, redecorating, cooking, and spending time with her grown children, their spouses, and new babies. She now had the house to herself all day but could fill it easily with friends and relatives whenever she wished. Her life was perfect. Mike was happy that she was happy but felt she did too much for everyone else and had little time and energy left for him. He came home at night and felt that his wife's world no longer included him in the same way. Things were changing, the focus of the marriage had somehow shifted. Then Mike announced he was taking the retirement package from his company and everything changed again. At first Janet was pleased because she thought Mike would become part of the world she had created for herself; Mike was just as sure that once he retired Janet would stop all that "running around" and concentrate on him. They were both wrong. Had they sat down and discussed their respective needs and expectations they would have been surprised to find that they were almost completely at odds about what lifestyle to adopt when Mike retired. Each simply assumed that the other would adapt. After all, being together was the point, wasn't it? The details didn't matter, everything would fall into place naturally. After all, they both said, hadn't they had to make major changes and adjustments when they married and blended all those kids? That had turned out just fine; so would this new development.

Now, several years later, they're getting divorced and probably still don't understand how it might have been prevented. Instead of adapting to each others' needs they rigidly guarded their own ideas of what life should be like. Mike wanted to do nothing—literally—and Janet wanted constant activity and involvement with family and friends. Mike was content to putter in the yard, sit on the beach, watch television, or read. Janet couldn't believe it. "How can you just do nothing all day?" was a question he felt no need to answer. He was happy just being home alone with her. He found the constant stream of visitors, both family and friends, intrusive and annoying. Janet viewed his lack of interest in hobbies, sports, or even part-time work as laziness and lack of character. There was no happy medium for either of them and it was clear from the phone call that they'd found the only solution they both agreed upon—divorce. Early counseling and planning might not have prevented their divorce but it might have given them a clearer picture of what each of them needed and a place to start trying to work it out.

When people retire, they do not mysteriously enter a vacuum, instead, they embark upon a cluster of relationships, the primary one being with their spouse. For years, as children grow and careers mature, couples often complain that they never have enough time to spend together. Then, as the years roll by—years of living together—the couple quickly discovers that retirement has left them with an abundance of time. Many couples understand that their relationship will change to some degree and that no human relationship can sustain such closeness twenty-four hours a day. Some couples do not realize this and don't make the necessary adjustments.

Retirement can make a revealing change in a couple's life and can lead to new irritations brought on by being together too much. Sometimes everything is done in unison: one spouse is rarely seen without the other. "Steve and Barb are inseparable," say their friends. A spouse may say, "We have each other," or "For the first time he really needs me." The relationship can become suffocating.

For some couples, the sense of being smothered is claustrophobic; the feeling of being paralyzed is overwhelming. This can cause either or both individuals to rebel and feel aggravated without realizing why. A husband may trace his wife's movement as she goes about her daily household chores. Sometimes he tries to be helpful, like alphabetizing the spice cabinet or making other superfluous infringements on her role. Even ideal marriages show signs of strain from this type of togetherness activity. The wife may say, "I care about John very much, but we are together constantly. Sometimes I just feel trapped and unable to breathe."

How can a person who feels imprisoned be a good life companion? The woman may say to her husband, "Today, I'm going to the library alone and then I'm going to stop at the mall." Sometimes this is accompanied by guilty feelings. The wife knows that her husband doesn't want to be alone. She feels uncomfortable about leaving him by himself. Then she thinks to herself, "I had to get out of the house and away from him for awhile. I told myself that he needs to find something to do. I am not going to be the answer to his loneliness." This whole scenario is usually accomplished by strong, ambivalent emotions.

Shelly is sixty-one and her husband, George, is sixty-five. He is a college graduate and has worked as a manager for a large, national consumer products company. His job kept him busy twelve hours a day; sometimes he worked weekends, and because he was so involved with work, Shelly raised their three children with very little help from George. George missed out on a lot. Six months ago, he retired and he never goes anywhere except with his wife. When she goes out, "He's my shadow," she commented, "and it's driving me crazy! The only place I can go without him is to the ladies-only church meeting. He has no interests. He hangs around the kitchen, lifts lids and stirs my pots on the stove, which drives me up the wall. When George was working, all his coworkers remarked on how pleasant he was and how he never got angry. Now he complains about almost everything and if he doesn't get his way, he has a tantrum—imagine, at his age. I am seriously considering a part-time job to get away from him."

Sometimes there are altercations, followed by reconciliations. On other occasions there are negotiations and then compromises. The difficulty can be expressed in different ways: the silent treatment, one or both partners ignoring the other, or a sharp tone of voice. When the emotional kettle boils over, it becomes a shouting match with slamming doors and verbal abuse.

There is a point to all this commotion and adjustment: no one can be *everything* to another person. If one partner tries or is expected to be everything and the situation continues too long, each partner depletes the other's emotional vigor and personal growth ceases altogether. What's left is little more than tolerance and coexistence. A balance must be developed between being together and being independent. Each spouse, it is hoped, will be able to use his or her own resources and common sense to reach a level of self-sufficiency without feeling threatened by the other's dependency.

Some spouses may have become emotionally detached because they were so busy every day that their partner's needs were not clearly perceived anymore. Worst of all, that unique feeling of two people being partners for life has almost disappeared and now life seems empty. As couples focus their attention on completing what needs to be done each day, they easily forget about one another. Personal needs for closeness, communication, and doing things together are neglected. Sometimes one of the partners "blows up," focusing on a variety of peripheral issues rather than the central problem: "You still, after all these years, don't replace the toilet paper roll when it runs out—you just leave it for me to do. You still haven't learned to close the cupboard doors or replace the toothpaste cap. Your irritating little habits continue. You hide behind your false pride by never admitting when you are obviously wrong—and when you hurt my feelings, it would be appropriate if you would say you're sorry. Most of the time you act like I'm not even here!"

Unfortunately, there are those who end up divorced, separated, or just continuously unhappy and miserable because they are unable to emerge successfully from this situation of mutual or one-sided intransigence; they never reach the ideal balance of stability and compromise that a satisfying relationship offers to sustain them both.

On the other hand, it is the way couples deal with differences and disagreements that can strengthen the relationship. Betty and George had had their problems throughout their twenty-eight years of marriage and, with retirement facing them in the next few years, they wanted to be sure they made every effort to improve their relationship. Both knew the transition from full-time work to retirement would be a bit more difficult than crossing the street. George's quick temper and Betty's confrontational pattern had been a classic recipe for unpleasant situations that, in the past, left each not speaking to the other for extended periods.

Betty and George felt that even in retirement, it was never too late to learn how to quarrel constructively and be practical about it. They knew that if they tried they could achieve safe ways to ventilate and discuss issues that might cause anxiety and concern and erupt in quarreling. Together they attended a seminar, "Safe Battles," sponsored by the local community college, where they were exposed to a number of useful suggestions. For example, they learned to set aside a specific time when both were free and able to discuss any problems. Having an objective mental attitude, such as "I'm sure we can resolve this with mutual understanding," came next. Allowing each spouse to talk without interruption, to permit the person a free discourse, they learned, regardless of how tempted the partner is to "chime in," is part of the process. Each partner needs to seriously listen, to sincerely try to understand the other's position, and to respond constructively without being patronizing.

Betty and George both agreed this was practical and logical as well as an approach each of them usually took in dealing with differences in their business environment; yet up to now, neither had the presence of mind to apply it to their own relationship. Though their retirement is only about one year away, both feel more enthusiastic about the future and their relationship because they've been practicing what they learned at the seminar. "It's beginning to work," they said. "We follow the process when those telltale signs to a provocative situation begin to rise. We found we can really solve our problems and there is no more 'I'm right this time and I'm going to win!' Wow, after twenty-eight years we're actually nourishing our relationship."

Sometimes partners discover that most of their conversation has been external: daily activities, work, the children's problems. With the onset of retirement, without these outside influences, couples are forced to be intimate, and for many it is difficult because they have been away from it for so long. It's like learning to fall in love all over again—with the same person. It takes time to readjust but it works out fine for many in retirement.

This is not the end of the possible difficulties. When, for example, the husband is not emotionally ready for retirement, the transition experience can be very painful. He is unprepared for the trauma that can result when he feels the loss of his identity now that his life lacks a supportive work environment, a structure, and familiar interpersonal relationships he's been used to all his working life. When this happens, the wife may take on the responsibility for her husband's failure to adjust to retirement, since she devotes a respectable amount of her time to managing her family's stresses and strains.

After years of being a decision maker in the competitive industry of advertising where power and achievement prompted a daily smile, Gordon remembered looking out of his corner office window of the fifty-fifth floor for the last time. Gordon chose early retirement eight months ago. "It all happened very quickly," he said. The company gave him four weeks to decide and he said yes. Suddenly Gordon, fifty-six years of age, was no longer a corporate executive. Now he judges that choice painfully: "I've kicked myself for doing it many times." Loyal and hard-working, seasoned at top companies, having considerable experience, but with nowhere to go, no project or problem to direct his eager energy toward, Gordon has a great deal of emotional baggage that he doesn't know what to do with and that he needs to put down somewhere.

Gordon's wife, Wendy, was consoling and understanding about her husband's feelings, thinking that after a few months he would redirect his energy and begin to think, "Well, I'm not the first person to feel this way about leaving a career and I won't be the last. I have to get on with my life." Unfortunately, that hasn't happened: after eight months of recalcitrant behavior on Gordon's part, Wendy has had to get on with her life. She tries to include Gordon in as many of her daily activities as possible and occasionally she sees a flicker of self-momentum from him. She has suggested that he consider teaching courses in advertising and sales promotion management at the state university in the next town. Wendy has picked up an application and the name of the professor Gordon should meet with. She hopes her husband will call him.

Often retired husbands look to their wives to fill empty and inactive days. Most husbands have never before had to deal with the question, "What will I do today?" This can be tremendously frustrating, especially for wives who are looking forward to their own retirement freedom. Not having children to care for and no longer acting as the family referee leaves them free to do the things they want to do with the rest of their lives. They find that their husbands want them to do something they don't wish to do anymore—be nurturers.

My wife and I had a brief discussion about this. We saw a cute baby, and I have to admit I'm a pushover for children. We have three, all of whom are almost grown. I half-jokingly said to her, "You know, I could go for another one, even now." My wife turned to me quite seriously and said, "That's not even amusing. I don't want to have to take care of anyone anymore. I'm tired of it."

Some men are unable to face their real feelings about retirement. Discussing their needs and feelings doesn't come easily; often they have no one with whom to share this crisis. Few men seek new friendships, even with other men, after retirement, and the relationships they do have with male friends are less giving than those with female friends.

The November 1987 issue of *Modern Maturity* magazine reported a study conducted by Dr. Karen Roberto of the University of Northern Colorado's gerontology program and Dr. Jean Pearson Scott of Texas Tech University. The study showed that with relationships later in life men tend to keep their friendships on a more surface level, whereas women's relationships are more intimate. Women seem to have more friends and place more value on them than men do. A married man's best friend is usually his wife; a woman's closest friend is another female. Therefore, husbands often have no one to unburden their frustrations on except their wives.

A wife needs to be sensitive to the changes her husband experiences, but she cannot be overprotective, because her husband is the only person who can solve his problems. If he understands he has his wife's support and love, he will ultimately draw on his own resources and make a satisfactory adjustment. At the same time, while being supportive when they are together, the wife needs to make sure that she takes time for herself.

There are many conflicts that couples can experience at this stage of life: problems with respect to personal identity; the need all of a sudden to develop new interests; the discord around changing roles with respect to work, spouse, or partner; and attempts to discern the road ahead. One thing is certain: the spousal relationship will change, but that keeps life interesting. Many of the difficulties can be avoided or certainly tempered.

Part of the solution is for the partners to become aware that the spousal relationship *will* change, and that both partners need to take the time to make plans for the future of their marriage. The couple has to develop a strategy for making this new, different, and changing part of life worthwhile, for each of them. Negotiating the way in which each will adapt to the changed situation can be complex and difficult, but certainly most couples should be able to bring it to a successful conclusion. One method with which to begin the process is for the couple facing retirement to sit down and discuss the expectations that each has of the other, or, even better, to develop a written outline. Writing can provide an initial vehicle for their expression. If both the husband and wife take the time, ahead of retirement, to be honest with each other and plan their future, the retirement years will provide considerable promise for both of them. Many find that they really can fall in love all over again—with the same person.

I always invite those people attending my workshops and speaking engagements to write to me about their pre- and postretirement experiences. In a way, it's one of the best ways to collect information about the realities of this midpoint in life and the transitions people go through. Karen and Mat wrote to me about a year after attending my two-day seminar sponsored by the company Mat worked for. Their letter expressed a lot of enthusiasm and revelations about what they had discovered about one another even though they had been married twenty-four years and were planning to retire within the next five. Karen and Mat wrote that they had followed my advice in my program and completed the exercise described above, in which both partners write down what they want from the other and from marriage in retirement over a period of time, a month for example. Be specific, I said, and go into detail about your expectations, as well as about your emotional, sexual, and physical needs. For many people, marriage during retirement continues to be emotionally and physically satisfying over the years, while for others, problems dog the relationship—problems a partner may never even have been aware of.

Karen and Mat wrote they had made a "date" for six weeks from the time they began writing to give themselves enough time, and they would have dinner at their favorite local restaurant. "We were excited and looking forward to that Saturday evening when both of us would bring our lists and discuss them. Each of us sort of had 'butterflies' in our stomach—we guessed it was from the anticipation of perhaps bringing out into the open some things we never fully discussed about each other and maybe finding out things we never knew. It was like a mini-adventure, something we had never thought about doing before and if we had, it never became a reality." After toasting one another with a glass of their favorite wine, Karen and Mat each unfolded their list. Karen began reading aloud what she had written. She felt that over the years they had let romance slip away and their responsiveness to each other and affectionate behaviors had waned. When their romantic interludes became a rarity, a lot of the intimacy between them diminished and Karen wanted some of it back. She felt that romance is emotionally meaningful at any age, and sometimes as people grow older, it requires a bit of extra effort to get back on the path to a little romance and attention. Karen told Mat that it was difficult to imagine there was a time years ago when they could increase their respiration just through a gentle touch or simply holding hands. Their last vacation had given her time to think, seeing some other couples about their own age acting like "kids." This, coupled with my workshop, brought back the memory of those old feelings and Karen realized she would give almost anything to feel that way again. She didn't want to spend the rest of her life without some of it. Karen's list also had a variety of other interesting suggestions, from things they could both do together in retirement to her own personal goals.

Mat was initially surprised at Karen's comments about the general decline of romance in their marriage; but instead of responding with a bland statement of how most couples' romantic attentiveness dwindles over the years, he realized Karen was correct and he missed it also. It seemed they both had become gradually accustomed to their present relationship; to change it, to "spark it," would require from each of them a conscious effort to do things differently to romance each other. The path of least resistance was to let things go on as they were. Mat and Karen planned to think of ways to get their relationship back to where they wanted it and it was going to be fun doing it—to sort of rediscover themselves!

Mat's list also had some ideas about things he and Karen could do together when they retired. Actually, Mat's main concern was that they wouldn't have a lot of time to spend together, since Karen wanted to teach a low-impact aerobics class to adults fifty years of age and over at the local YWCA. Mat wanted a partner in retirement while Karen seemed interested in becoming involved in something that would limit their time together. After realistically looking at how much time Karen would spend teaching and the total amount of time available in retirement, Mat realized he was overreacting. Karen agreed with her husband that the first priority was their feelings about each other and a positive partnership.

This is a good example of how two people approached their future retirement in an objective and open way to identify their concerns and to express their feelings along with suggestions on working toward a common goal. By doing this before retirement, neither Karen nor Mat became defensive and there was very little pressure. It was an education process about many aspects of their relationship.

In busy marriages and lifestyles, it's easy to touch only when there is sexual interest. Affectionate, nonsexual touching is something couples drift away from as they get older, but this type of contact several times each day reaffirms the emotional bond between two people.

Some couples rediscover each other after the children leave home. Relaxed styles, reduced stress, more leisure time together, increased focus on each other, and fewer financial worries often lead to rekindled romance, intimacy, and sexual vitality. Partners communicate more with each other, and are more understanding and tolerant. This can lead to a relationship that combines the romance of a young married couple with the comforts of close friends. Romance in adulthood and retirement is the type of experience that helps keep people youthful. It doesn't have to disappear with age; it is too important a part of life's quality.

When my doctor of thirty years, Al Greene, announced that he was thinking about retirement I realized that there are a few professions where people seem to retire late or not at all. Judges, politicians, actors and actresses, and doctors, to name a few, always seem to be working into their seventies or even eighties. Why? What is it about these jobs that keeps people wanting to work? To keep away from a spouse? I doubt it. What happens when they do retire? Do they experience more or less stress than others who retired at a more traditional age? I didn't know anybody in the other professions, but I did know my doctor. To help me answer these questions, Dr. Greene agreed to a sort of ongoing study of his retirement beginning ten years ago with his decision to leave his active practice after forty years and continuing at selected intervals along the way. This impromptu investigation began when Dr. Greene started to rethink his plans to continue working non-stop for the rest of his life. I was curious about the reasons for this reappraisal, as I knew his practice was sound, his health good, and his marriage happy. He put it this way:

> Guild, I had achieved everything I always thought I wanted: success in my field, the recognition and respect of my colleagues, a comfortable lifestyle, and a happy marriage. There were no surprises left, no more obstacles to overcome, and no further professional goals to strive for. I realized that my whole life had been directed by my pursuit of a medical career and driven by my desire to contribute to society in a meaningful way. Somewhere in this long, hard climb I had lost

myself. I no longer knew what made *me* happy. I rarely thought about it, actually, until asked by a young colleague what my plans were for retirement. He had his already worked out and he was twenty years my junior! I was startled to discover that I had no idea of life beyond medicine. I was certainly in a position to understand that old age could result in certain incapacitating conditions which might, in fact, leave me unable to continue practicing medicine at all or in some diminished capacity. That young man made me think and I'm very glad he did.

At that point ten years ago, Dr. Greene began to look around at what other people were doing about planning their retirement. As the options unfolded, he realized he wanted to retire while he was still active and healthy, not when he was forced by circumstances. Dr. Greene was fortunate to have the time and resources he needed to thoroughly research retirement. This became his new goal and he welcomed the challenge. Because he had been so busy with his medical practice, he hadn't had the opportunity to be much of a companion to his wife other than on their annual vacations. He hoped to change that.

Before his retirement Dr. Greene and his wife, Betty, decided to systematically review their vacation choices of the last five years and to see whether or not there was a pattern to how they spent their precious leisure time. They discovered they were most often drawn to the southern coastal areas—the low country. They enjoyed the balmy weather, the ocean, the golf course, and the slower pace of life. They agreed that their trips south always left them feeling refreshed and renewed. That revelation led to the purchase of a vacation home near Savannah, Georgia, a city they both loved. They spent time there during each season to get a complete picture of what life might be like there for them all year round. With the location decided, they turned their attention to the question of what would occupy their days after Dr. Greene—I'll call him Al now—became just another retiree. Could anything be as demanding or as fulfilling or prestigious as being a physician? It was at this point that their life began literally going to the dogs.

It began when Betty's mother, Claire, moved in with them. She was getting older and was alone after the death of Betty's father several years before. Having lived all her life in a city apartment, Claire found her daughter's large suburban home isolated and a little frightening, especially when she had to be there alone. Betty thought a puppy would be the ideal solution. It would require a lot of attention, provide companionship and, when grown, offer at least the illusion of protection. Years before Claire had had a Scotty she loved, so Al and Betty felt that would be the most appropriate choice again. For most people the next step would have been the local pet shop. However, Betty and Al were methodical about everything and they approached the purchase of the puppy as they would anything else: they researched it. Thus began for Al and Betty, from the simple decision to buy a dog, an odyssey of discovery not only about Scotties but about themselves and a glimpse of what life in retirement might be like for them.

From the moment "MacGregor" entered their lives everything was different. He had been purchased from a breeder in the next state recommended to them by the American Kennel Club. The day Al and Betty went to pick him up they were excited in a way they had never expected to be. It was like going to adopt a child. They had a basket, food, tags, the kennel, all the necessary equipment, and had read several books the breeder had sent ahead. They were ready. The moment they saw him they were hooked. That small, wiggly, black bundle changed their lives. Claire was thrilled with her gift and content now to be at home caring for her puppy. A whole new world was about to open for Al and Betty, and it had nothing whatsoever to do with Al's medical career or Betty's charity work. They found themselves immersed in classes to learn how to show MacGregor at dog shows, and papers to look over and file with the American Kennel Club. They joined a local Scottish Terrier club and so discovered a whole group of like-minded people to socialize with.

Soon, one dog was just not enough for three people to share, so they began a second round of searching for a puppy. "Mary" soon joined them and shortly after came "Piper." As the dogs grew and were entered in more and more shows and produced several litters of puppies, Al and Betty thought more and more of retiring to devote themselves full-time to breeding and showing these wonderful dogs. What had begun as a diversion for Claire had blossomed into a lifestyle all three enjoyed. Eventually, the dogs won out and Al retired. He and Betty and Claire now live full-time in Savannah with fifteen Scotties who have the run of their sprawling plantation-style house. They have found a new life together that they share with equal joy—from going to dog shows to grooming to cleaning up. Their relationship has not only survived retirement, it has a new excitement and sparkle that comes from truly appreciating each other and sharing common goals as they enjoy their retirement adventure.

Couples need to discuss their plans and aspirations long before the retirement process begins, at least five years ahead of time. It requires more than a few superficial talks. Sometimes preparation takes years, but the planning can be challenging and enjoyable. Passivity and ignorance will not secure a compatible and productive future relationship that will sustain a couple for the rest of their lives. But what a wonderful time of life this is. It requires a commitment, an investment in time, and honest communication. It's part of the adventure!

At one of my recent retirement workshops in upstate New York, I smiled to myself as I overheard a woman say to her husband during the break period, "How wonderful that you're retiring, honey," trying to sound cheerful. "You deserve to take it easy. After all, you've been working since you were about eight years old. Now you can repair the house and do all the things you always wanted to do. I won't have to get up early to make your breakfast, so I can retire, too." They were both looking at each other with big grins on their faces anticipating their new adventure together.

7

"How Long Do You Want to Live?"

"Have a good sense of humor. Don't complain all the time. Be a good listener and let others talk. Never argue, because it could be bad for the blood pressure. Have at least one cocktail at four o'clock."

"I expect to live to be one hundred because I exercise every day, I'm careful about the foods I put into my body, and I keep mentally active. I work at it. I'm in better health now than before I retired."

During a recent national speaking tour on the importance of retirement planning, the majority of those attending my presentation responded to the question, "What do you consider the most important factor contributing to a successful and happy retirement?" with the answer "good health." When the same people were asked, "To what age would you like to live?" usually everyone just looked at me without answering. They were incredulous because no one had ever asked them that question before. Inevitably I had to repeat the question and this time I usually received responses such as sixty-eight, seventy-three, or eighty-five.

When I asked the attendees their biggest concerns about retirement, most responded by saying they were worried about losing their physical and/or mental health. They feared living long after being able to function independently.

This reminds me of the Chinese proverb, "Man fools himself. He prays for a long life and then he fears old age." There is a mistaken belief that old age inevitably leads to illness and that there is a direct relationship between aging and finding oneself confined to a rocking chair, a walker, or a nursing home. Aging in our society has frequently been equated with decline because American culture clings to some very pessimistic assumptions about aging. Growing old is often associated with frailty, sickness, and loss of vitality. Many people in their fifties and sixties are resigned to the fallacy that added years mean restricted physical mobility and, eventually, decreased mental activity. Let's be clear about one thing: aging is not a disease.

There are retired people who do not feel old, and old people who never retire, but many people think about the fact that they are getting older around the time they start to consider retirement. If they are not careful, these folks may tend to perceive the two—being retired and being old—as identical. If this occurs, such individuals may link the various adjustments of retirement to the dawning of old age, thereby creating a self-fulfilling prophecy about the consequences of both.

Most people believe that there is nothing they can do about aging. Their strategy for facing this unpleasant prospect is, first, to deny their own decline into old age, and then to resign themselves to the progressive deterioration of mental and physical capacities. All sorts of false conclusions emerge about what happens to them, especially if their perception of retirement and old age is one that includes eventual infirmity.

Older persons who find themselves in situations in which they can't remember something may say, "What can I expect? I'm getting old and my memory isn't as sharp as it once was." The same people at thirty-five would have said, "I should have written that down."

When relatively young people experience soreness in legs and arms after playing softball for the first time in five years, they may exclaim, "Boy, am I stiff, but it feels good to get back to playing." Those same people at age fifty-five might say, "This old body isn't what it used to be." Thirty-year-olds who get a cramp when jogging would say, "I got a charley horse." Those in their sixties may say, "I'm too old for this: my joints are wearing out and my muscles stiffen up a lot."

It seems some folks are afraid to think in terms of being active and healthy in their sixties, seventies, eighties, nineties, and beyond. It also seems that the fear of being old and infirm is what prevents many from being old and healthy. For example, people will say, "Oh, at my age I wouldn't dream of doing . . . ," or "Don't be foolish, at my age I no longer am able to. . . ." Too many older Americans think about aging as a gradually constricting circle of fewer mental and physical experiences. They believe that as they become older, their physical capabilities will be limited and their mental ability impaired. Too many simply give up. But there is a lot we can do about how we age. Some people have represented their lifespan as a bell curve, maturing to comfort and prosperity, only to deteriorate into disability and dependency. Aging is part of our natural growth process, so why can't it be exciting and forceful to the end?

Too often, older people have made truth of the fables about aging by failing to maintain or improve their health. Many people perpetuate the self-fulfilling prophecy of "growing old." They act old, sound old, and think old. Gerontophobia, that dreadful fear of growing old we've already talked about, seems to be inherent in many people because we directly or indirectly are taught the fear: old is unattractive, weak, forgetful, dependent, near death—and we definitely fear death! Advancing age is not an irreversible condition in which our bodies wear out. In most people, it is possible to change the body's condition regardless of age or the former lack of exercise and sound eating habits. It is possible to regain vitality, muscular strength, and aerobic endurance whether a person is fifty-five or eighty-five. We don't need to subscribe to the falsehood that aging is synonymous with diminished capacities. The active, nourished mind remains sharp, alert, and productive, and the active, nourished body retains its elasticity, strength, and normal range of movement.

Far too many people assume that older persons are a burden to the community, to their families, and even to themselves. While some aged people are in need of varying degrees of public and private assistance, the fact remains that a great many older individuals lead satisfying lives and maintain their health well beyond society's expectations.

People should establish a health-related objective for themselves, for example, "I'm going to make regular exercise a central part of my life and work my other activities around exercise." Most people have been conditioned to think health is too complicated, that an expert's help is needed. But often the most simple of strategies can yield the most impressive benefits. What is the advantage of a longer lifespan if you're too ill and debilitated to enjoy older life? In an article in the May 1992 *Better Homes and Gardens* titled "Stay Young (Almost) Forever!" Gene Cohen, M.D., Ph.D., former acting director of the National Institute on Aging, says, "Dull as they may sound, the keys to successful aging are ample exercise, good nutrition, and healthy lifestyle habits. These things will slow down the aging process better than any longevity drug."

Getting back to my workshop, I asked the participants another important question: "Is living as long as you possibly can—whether it be to age 95 or 105—provided you're healthy and reasonably independent, a rational objective?" The unanimous response was always yes.

I believe the vast majority of people feel this way, though some may quietly reject the idea of living past the century mark. Nonetheless, many Americans do want to live to be one hundred. A 1993 nationwide survey by the nonprofit Alliance for Aging Research revealed that two out of three Americans say they would like to live a hundred years. Americans have high expectations about their longevity and 67 percent of those polled believe science will find ways to extend the average human life. In fact, this nation's longevity is rapidly increasing. The Population Reference Bureau, a private nonprofit research group in Washington, D.C., reported in 1993 that today's twenty-year-olds can expect to live an additional 56.6 years, 3.5 more years than those who turned twenty in the year 1970. That is a significant increase in just over two decades.

The federal government reported in 1993 that as of 1991, average life expectancy at birth had risen from the previous record of 75.4 years to 75.5 years, up by 0.1 years. The figure becomes more meaningful when this life expectancy is compared to that of 46 years in 1900. In this century, life expectancy has increased by almost thirty years. Lifespan, or the length of time we have the capacity to live from birth to death, is 110 years. According to Dr. Robert Butler, the first director of the National Institute on Aging, some researchers are even saying that 120 is certainly reasonable because there are people living that long and even longer. For example, the 1993 edition of the *Guiness Book of World Records* lists Shigechiyo Isumi of Asan, Japan, as being over 120 years old. There are others recorded to have lived to be that old; one Arthur Reed died at 124.

Today the fastest-growing population group is the eighty-five and older segment, and their numbers will increase sevenfold by 2050. In 1900, there were thirty-one people on record as being one hundred years old or over; in 1960, there were three thousand in the United States who had reached or passed their one hundredth milestone. In 1980, there were over 32,000 centenarians reported in the United States

Census, and in 1990, about 64,000; 210 people were turning one hundred every day. There may well be over a million Americans one hundred years old or over within the next fifty years. In his book *We Live Too Short and Die Too Long,* Dr. Walter M. Bortz II, one of America's most respected and acclaimed authorities on aging, says that today's centenarians are simply living the healthy, active, natural lifespan of one hundred years that the human body was designed to achieve, and many people can live far beyond what is expected.

One member of the audience at a recent workshop I conducted took exception to my comment that many older people live quality lives. He remarked that his eighty-eight-year-old mother was in a nursing home and had little quality of life. "She has few choices now, if any, and I think the majority of older people, particularly those one-hundred-year-olds you refer to, are being kept alive on respirators and other life-sustaining machines."

This man was understandably upset about his own personal situation; but it's a fact that older people who are severely disabled are simply more likely to stand out. Our eyes are drawn, for example, to the eighty-year-old invalid in a wheelchair. We are oblivious of the octogenarian who vigorously walks by because that person mixes in with everyone else. However, many observers have a tendency to create an erroneous image about older folks because it fits their expectations, their perceptions of what a person eighty, ninety, or one hundred is supposed to be like.

I have seen people fifty years old who function as if they were ninety and infirm. Even some forty-year-olds are physically aged because of poor genes, an unhealthy lifestyle, or plain bad luck.

Many, many older people are living life fully and having a delightful time. One S. L. Potter, at age one hundred, made his first bungee jump from a 210-foot tower in Alpine, California. In seeking to become the world's oldest bungee jumper, Potter ignored the advice of his daughter and three sons, who themselves range in age from sixty-eight to seventy-four. They were fearful that he would die in flight.

"It's possible," Potter admitted before the leap. "If I die, I die. I told everybody to bring a shovel and a mop, just in case."

Here are some more examples of active seniors:

Ed McCarty of Kimberley, Idaho, was born in 1900, yet he still flies his rebuilt thirty-year-old Ercoupe airplane at the age of ninety-four.

Harry Stevens of Beloit, Wisconsin, was 103 when he married Thelma Lucas, 84.

Griffith Williams of Llithfaen, Great Britain, published his autobiography on his 102nd birthday on June 5, 1990.

At the age of eighty-seven Norman Vaughn recently completed his fifth 1,100 mile Iditarod Trail dog sled race from Anchorage to Nome, Alaska.

Centenarian Teiichi Igarashi and ninety-one-year-old Hulda Crooks both climbed Japan's Mount Fuji, which is 12,385 feet high.

Milton and Marga Feher, a couple in their eighties, manage a dance studio in New York that offers classes specially for older students. One of their star pupils is 103-year-old Clair Willi, who took her first dance class when she was in her seventies.

The Sun City Pom Poms—average age seventy-three—started cheerleading fourteen years ago for an all-girls baseball team. Now the Sun City, Arizona, women whoop it up all over the nation. Not even knee operations or hip replacements can keep these spirited seniors from performing cartwheels and tap dance routines. "Sometimes our bones are aching and we have to drag ourselves to the field," says Pom Pom Helen Sisko, age seventy-three, "but when we hear the crowds roar, we forget our aches and pains. I guess we're all a bunch of hams!"

Gladys Cassidy of Dravosberg, Pennsylvania, was ninety when she entered her first beauty contest—Ms. Pennsylvania Senior. For the pageant's talent competition, she performed a hip-swinging hula dance that brought down the house. "Every age has its rewards," Gladys said. "When you're ninety, you can dye your hair, act the fool, do anything you want—and other people just enjoy you." Gladys won second place.

"I'm not happy unless I have a challenge," says Peggy Parr, "and that hasn't changed just because I'm eighty-one." From the ages of fifty-eight to sixty-six, the Colorado Springs woman performed 240 rescue missions as part of a mountain rescue squad, each of which was no small feat: she had to be lowered from helicopters by a rope in high winds, and then carry injured hikers down rocky cliffs. Now Peggy hikes twenty-five miles a week and still scrambles up any rock face that looks interesting. "If you sit at home and say, 'I'm old and tired,' you get old and tired," she says.

Isabella Cannon had been retired only a few weeks when she told herself, "Isabella, you need to get up and get on with the rest of your life." She's been doing that ever since. At seventy-three, she was elected mayor of Raleigh, North Carolina, and today, at eighty-six, she remains one of the city's best-known citizens.

You could say that every letter carried by Don Taylor is a special delivery. At age ninety-eight, he's the country's oldest mailman, having begun his career delivering mail to ranchers of eastern Wyoming in 1943. He's not actually employed by the Post Office but works as an independent carrier under a rural mail delivery contract that comes up for renewal in 1995—one year before his hundredth birthday!

Helene Schaefer, a grandmother of fifteen and great-grandmother of seven, received her Master of Fine Arts degree from Manhattanville College in Purchase, New York, just three months shy of her ninetieth birthday. She graduated with a B-plus average.

If your objective is to live as long as possible, or "life extension with quality," how can you achieve it? The premise of wellness is that you can live a long, healthy, and active life. Provided you're in good health to begin with, all you need is the desire to do so, and the right information on which to base your actions. Time marches on and no one can stop it, but you don't have to accept aging as a negative aspect of life. In fact, you can take steps to keep yourself feeling, looking, and acting younger, no matter how old you get.

Aging is a process with many factors. It is characterized by a progressive deterioration in physical performance and an increasing tendency toward the development of degenerative diseases, including coronary artery and heart disease, hypertension, stroke, diabetes, and cancer. However, the evidence is mounting that these diseases may be attributable far more to lifestyle than the biological aging process. Unfortunately, many Americans become sedentary and adopt poor eating habits as they become older, which is one reason that few people in America die healthy although the overwhelming majority are born healthy. Chronic illness and disability need not be constant companions of older people if a positive lifestyle is adopted or, as one woman said at one of my seminars, we practice "smart living."

Many of us feel that if we have our health, we can do just about anything. But good health is rarely a happy accident; most of us have to work at it. Although we cannot change our genetic makeup, we can control many aspects of our lives that may lead to a longer life free from the common fears of aging.

It is estimated that only 1 to 3 percent of the annual health care bill in the United States goes for preventive services such as research into the cause rather than the cure of some diseases like prostate and breast cancer, the importance of good nutrition, and education to improve personal health habits. As a society we encourage researchers to look for drugs as the solution instead of changing our lifestyle and preventing the problem from occurring in the first place. People's habits and choices can do more than the entire medical establishment; however, most Americans believe that medical care is the key to health: "Do whatever you want right now—the doctor will fix it later on." If people accept that myth, they will fail to invest in the personal actions that pay off in being healthier and in feeling and looking better.

Think about how you want to look at age sixty, seventy, eighty, and beyond, and about what you want to be able to do. The way you spend your time now will determine how you are engaged in those later years. You have the choice of creating a truly healthy, vibrant extended life for yourself. When "maturity" includes an openness to healthful lifestyle changes, many of the physical and mental ills once blamed completely on aging can be alleviated or postponed.

We need to take charge of our own health because no one is going to do it for us; we need to "live smart." This process of smart living comprises exercise, nutrition, medical screenings, and a second half of life of meaningful activity, all of which are discussed in the following chapters.

8

Exercise Works Wonders

"I'm so damn happy and satisfied with my retiremeat, I sometimes wonder if I'm becoming senile. The fact is that I attribute this to maintaining a very active and healthy lifestyle. My daily exercise not only has kept me physically fit with a healthy body but it makes a difference in my mental outlook as well."

"For years I knew that I should be more active and exercise regularly. I set goals for my business to increase sales but I failed setting goals to increase the chances for good health. I am now paying the price for my lack of discipline."

Hardly a day goes by when we are not reminded to walk, jog, swim, or take aerobic classes. The case for exercise grows each day, particularly as people get older. Research is yielding very tangible evidence of its dramatic benefits, as you will discover when reading this chapter.

Why not begin by answering the following questions about health and exercise? Then, as you proceed through this chapter, you may begin to develop new ideas about how the information contained in it can impact your own future.

1. A recent study by the U.S. Centers for Disease Control and Prevention analyzed the leisure-time physical activities of over 87,000 adults, revealing that what percentage of the fifty-five and older age group was sedentary:
   (a) 82 percent

97

    (b) 62 percent
    (c) 49 percent

2. What is the best measure of a person's physical fitness?
    (a) How good your body looks
    (b) How much blood your heart can pump
    (c) How physically strong you are
    (d) How much oxygen your body can consume
    (e) How much body fat you have

3. Which three words best describe experts' recommendations for physical activity?
    (a) Brisk, sustained, and regular
    (b) Relaxed, repetitive, and paced
    (c) Enjoyable, energetic, and selective
    (d) Short, rapid, and maximized

4. Which of the following will best motivate a person to continue with a fitness program?
    (a) "You're doing just great—keep it up!"
    (b) "Exercise will make you healthier and provide a better chance for a longer life."
    (c) "Nature meant the human body to be healthy and fit."
    (d) "You owe it to those you love and who depend on you."
    (e) "Your blood pressure decreased 2 percent over the past month."

5. Exercise reduces the risk associated with which of the following diseases?
    (a) Colon and breast cancer
    (b) Diabetes
    (c) Hypertension
    (d) Stroke
    (e) Heart disease
    (f) Osteoporosis

6. During the past year, which of the following have you done to improve your health and quality of life (note all that apply)?
Exercised regularly   _____
Lost weight   _____
Taken vitamins   _____
Gained weight   _____

Stopped drinking   _____
Stopped smoking   _____
Eaten more nutritiously   _____
Nothing   _____
Other   _____

Answers to questions 1 through 5:
Question 1: (b); Question 2: (d); Question 3: (a); Question 4: (e); Question 5: (a, b, c, d, e, and f)

"I spent half my life developing my brain and trying to achieve. Then I got close to retirement age and discovered that the quality of my life isn't what it should be because my body isn't in good shape." This quote comes from a written response to one of my recent research projects about retirement.

Our bodies, of course, don't come with a warranty, but what many people describe as problems of aging are really lifestyle issues. Many of the problems blamed on old age are not due to aging at all, but, rather, as we have discussed, to improper care of the body over a lifetime. A body that is properly maintained will show the effects of aging mildly and gradually. Some experts estimate that half the functional losses people experience are attributable to lack of exercise. In fact, the National Institutes of Health has declared exercise the most effective anti-aging method. Exercise is one of the best things you can do for your health. "If exercise could be packaged into a pill, it would be the most widely prescribed, and most beneficial medicine in the United States," notes Robert N. Butler, M.D., former director of the National Institute on Aging. Regular, moderate exercise—just three or four brisk thirty-minute walks each week, for example—has been shown to inhibit, arrest, or even reverse deficiencies in blood circulation, muscle power, lung capacity, bone mass, carbohydrate metabolism, and the speed at which messages travel from the brain to the nerve endings (known as reaction time). Exercise serves as a powerful defense against heart disease, osteoporosis, and high blood pressure. It helps control cholesterol, tone muscles and skin, improve regularity, maintain a desirable weight, relieve stress, and reduce the risk of depression and social withdrawal.

Studies show that some type of long-term aerobic exercise helps older people keep mentally sharp. Researchers at the Medical College of Pennsylvania are finding that older people who have exercised regularly score significantly higher than nonexercisers of the same age and intelligence on tests measuring recall and mental quickness. Regular aerobic exercise seems not only to help preserve neurological functioning into old age, but also to enhance it in older people who have been sedentary.* This is a good argument against the historical view that brain degeneration is inevitable.

Another study of fifty-five-to-seventy-year-olds at the Veterans Administration Medical Center in Salt Lake City found that those who took one-hour walks three times a week over a four-month period improved their reaction time, visual organization, and memory over others who remained sedentary. Increased circulation of oxygen and blood, as well as changes in the brain's biochemistry, probably accounted for these improvements.†

No matter how modest the routine or how late in life it is begun, an exercise program can always have health benefits. Exercise doesn't have to be grim and punishing to yield important benefits. The key is consistency rather than intensity. The first step is to consult with your physician before you begin. Next, simply find an activity you can enjoy and do on a regular basis. It can be as simple as taking regular walks. It's difficult to injure yourself walking and you can burn more calories by briskly walking than by jogging. As a person gets older, aerobic activity should be supplemented with strength training (discussed later in this chapter). Keep in mind that it is important to start slowly to avoid injury or the kind of unnecessary soreness that is likely to stifle initial enthusiasm.

A study completed by the Stanford University School of Medicine found that regular exercise is crucial to longevity. This survey of Harvard alumni found that those who walked five to ten miles a week reduced their mortality rate by about 10 percent. For those who walked up to twenty-five miles each week, the rate of death was lowered by almost 40 percent. This can mean a life extension of ten to twenty years. Experts say that a half hour of running or brisk walking, three times a week,

---

*Gary Yanker and Kathy Burton, *Walking Medicine* (New York: McGraw-Hill, 1993).

†University of California, Berkeley, *The Wellness Encyclopedia* (Boston: Houghton Mifflin, 1991).

is enough to decrease the average person's chances of dying from heart disease, cancer, stroke, and other major causes of death by about 50 percent.*

Another study reported in the November 3, 1989, issue of the *Journal of the American Medical Association* was one of the most extensive yet on the effects of fitness on longevity. The researchers, working at the Institute for Aerobic Research in Dallas, Texas, looked at more than 13,000 people for an average of eight years. It found that the least fit group (who were also the most sedentary) had significantly higher mortality rates than any other of the groups. The death rate dropped most sharply in those who exercised moderately, by 60 percent for men and 48 percent for women. To be in this group, the researchers estimated, all a person would have to do is walk briskly for thirty to sixty minutes every day. The study included 3,100 women who were found to benefit as much as the men from being fit. The data in this study were adjusted statistically to make sure that the higher mortality rate was due to lack of fitness and not other important risk factors, such as age, smoking, family history of heart disease, and high cholesterol or blood pressure.

In terms of longevity, a little exercise goes a long way, and more exercise may go even further. You don't need to be a marathon runner to reap the benefits of exercise. Studies show that the greatest leap in longevity was found in those who shifted from sedentary habits to engaging in low levels of exercise (such as brisk walking) for thirty minutes three or four days a week. Researchers also found that strenuous exercise improved the body's ability to break down life-threatening blood clots by increasing levels of a clot-dissolving protein called tissue plasminogen activator (TPA). TPA, which is produced naturally by cells in the blood vessels, can also be manufactured in the laboratory and can lessen damage to the heart muscle when administered quickly following a heart attack. But if natural levels of TPA are high, as they tend to be in younger people, or can be boosted, they may help to prevent a heart attack in the first place.

Many scientists believe exercise can actually reverse some effects of aging. In a landmark 1990 study, Dr. Maria Fiatarone and her colleagues at the Hebrew Rehabilitation Center for the Aged in Boston reported a reduction in the physical frailty of older people who

---

*The Johns Hopkins Medical Letter, Health After 50, February 1994.

participated in a regular exercise program. In this eight-week study, supported by Tufts University and the U.S. Department of Agriculture's Human Nutrition Research Center on Aging, ten frail men and women ranging in age from eighty-six to ninety-six regularly exercised their legs using a weight machine. The ten people in the original program had an average of 4.5 chronic diseases each and had been institutionalized for an average of 3.4 years. Eight had a history of falls and seven habitually used a cane or walker. The participants worked out three days a week, performing three sets consisting of a specific number of repetitions of leg lifts with a designated amount of weight; a one- or two-minute rest occurred between sets. The weight was gradually increased as muscles grew stronger. At the beginning of the study, the participants could lift only seventeen pounds per leg on average. By the end of the two months, they could lift an average of forty-five pounds! This is remarkable in light of their advanced age, extremely sedentary habits, multiple chronic diseases, functional disabilities, and nutritional inadequacies. After only two months, most had doubled their walking speed and could rise from a chair without using their arms for the first time in years. The importance of this study is that it shows how, even at an advanced age, physical frailty can be prevented or reversed. Because it was so successful, the study had been extended to more than 1,500 volunteers, some of whom are over one hundred years of age.

This leads us now into a discussion of broadening an exercise program. Aerobic exercises such as running, which use the large muscle groups to enhance cardiovascular endurance, are the cornerstone of fitness programs, but there must also be emphasis on the other elements of fitness, which are overall strength, flexibility and agility. People who focus only on aerobic activity—which has the extensive health benefits already discussed, including building up the leg muscles—may lose muscle mass in the upper body.

As most people past middle age can attest, muscle strength increases during early adulthood, levels off at around thirty-five to forty, and thereafter begins to decline in those who do not engage in muscle-strengthening activity. In fact, after the age of thirty, a sedentary individual may very well lose muscle fiber at the rate of 3 to 5 percent each decade, leading to a 30 percent diminishment of muscle power by the age of sixty.*

Overwhelmed by the aerobic trend of the past two decades, Americans have underestimated the importance of strengthening exercises. The American College of Sports Medicine altered its exercise training guidelines a few years ago for the first time in twelve years to include strength training along with aerobic exercises for healthy adults. It recommends resistance training (weight lifting) of moderate intensity at least twice a week: a minimum of eight to ten exercises involving the major muscle groups, each one repeated eight to twelve times. This shouldn't be intimidating, since it can take as few as fifteen minutes each session. The resistance can be provided by weight machines, dumbbells, or barbells. Dumbbells and barbells of various weights are relatively safe, but well-constructed weight machines, where the person is seated or lying down, offer the ultimate for seniors. Furthermore, since weights are held in place by pins and other constraints, there is no danger of having the weight fall. Most machines start with weights as low as two and a half to five pounds and move up incrementally from there, so it's easy for anyone to begin a program. Using one's own body weight and doing pushups, pullups, and bent leg situps is a satisfactory alternative to weights. The goal is not progressive body building—it's to find your own optimum level and then maintain it throughout life.

Our bodies are designed to be used. We weren't made to sit behind desks or dashboards, but we do. Life has become so convenient that we even let our fingers do the walking on certain occasions. We have to make a special effort to use our bodies the way they were meant to be used. When we think about it, humans evolved on the move, but many people don't do a lot of moving these days. The average person sits down to breakfast, and then sits in the car, bus, or train going to work. At work many sit at a desk or console; they then return home to sit down to dinner and to watch television; and then they lie down to sleep. That is a considerable amount of low-level physical activity.

Are you still sitting there making excuses for not getting enough exercise? Perhaps this will give you the nudge you need to change your ways. The American Heart Association has ranked physical inactivity

---

*Harvard Health Letter, July 1993.

right up there with cigarette smoking, high blood pressure, and high cholesterol levels as a major risk factor for heart disease. The AHA also affirms the relationship between physical inactivity and death from heart disease. It adds that people who exercise regularly after a heart attack live longer.

The effect of lifestyle factors has occasionally been given a hard time by academic researchers who cite the need for statistical analysis. Now several large studies give good evidence of a positive role for exercise. The February 1993 issue of the *New England Journal of Medicine* reported one study from Norway that followed more than 1,650 men for over twenty years. Another, from Harvard University, surveyed over 10,000 graduates and followed them for almost twenty years. Both reports cite significant reductions in earlier death and disability for those who exercise than for those who do not exercise. In fact, the study found that, for the most part, the more a person exercises, the better are his chances to outlive his peers. For example, during the years of observation men who walked nine or more miles a week had a 21 percent lower mortality rate than those who walked three miles a week or less.

Think about this: Nonexercisers' hearts beat (at rest) about 28,000 more times each day or 10,620,000 more times each year than the hearts of those who do exercise regularly. Or this: Nonexercisers spend twice as much in medical claims as exercisers do.* The evidence is overwhelming—exercise!

For most people, finding the motivation ("I want to live longer with a better quality of life" or "Not everything I do now will matter five years from now, but keeping my arteries healthy will") to begin exercising is not the problem; what's difficult is finding the discipline to continue with it. Research has documented the obvious: If people don't enjoy the activities they do, they discontinue them. In one study in the June 16, 1992, issue of *Journal of Applied Social Psychology,* participants in an exercise program were followed for six weeks. Those who engaged in an activity assigned to them had double the dropout rate of those who were able to choose an activity for themselves.

If you have trouble starting or staying with an exercise program,

*Ismail Corrigan and R. J. Young, "The Effects of Habitual Exercise on General Health as Reflected by Non-Accidental Insurance Claims," in *Sports Cardiology International Conference Magazine* (Bologna: Aulo Gaggi, 1988).

find something you enjoy. Better yet, choose several activities you enjoy and switch from one to another as the mood strikes you. Aim for a reasonable short-term fitness goal, such as walking twenty minutes this week and then building on it gradually, perhaps by adding five minutes a week. Make your goals attainable and specific. Once you have established your goals, make time to achieve them. Plan your exercise activity first, then work around that and fill in the rest of your activities. Many of us manage our lives by making appointments for almost everything, so approach exercise that way, or it may get left out. If you must cancel some daily activities for other commitments, keep exercise in and compromise something else. As in business, a partner can be an important asset to your workout program, so try to encourage someone to exercise with you.

Charting your progress by keeping records is essential, just as keeping records in business is. Maintaining some kind of record helps in two ways: 1) it focuses attention on what you're doing, and 2) it encourages you with visible results of your progress. It is very motivational to be able to look back over the weeks and months (and eventually years) to see how your own efforts have led to increased personal health and happiness. For example, you and your partner have planned to begin walking at the local high school track every other day, gradually accelerating each week the pace of walking and increasing the distance by one quarter mile, or once around the track, every two weeks until you're walking at least thirty minutes each session. You're both sure to take your resting pulse rate when you begin the program and also at the beginning of each week, being careful to mark it on a chart you have outlined. How will the progress be reflected by you and your partner? By the lowering of your resting pulse rate, since brisk walking will increase aerobic fitness levels and help make the heart a more efficient cardiac mechanism over a period of time.

In a May 13, 1991, *Newsweek* magazine article, Dr. Neil Gordon, director of exercise physiology at the Institute for Aerobics Research in Dallas, Texas, said: "As a matter of fact, you can turn back the hands of time." As startling as the idea sounds, it is not the passage of years that causes people to age. "We now understand that what we have ascribed to aging is simply for the most part due to inactivity," says Dr. Stanley Birge, director of the program on aging at Washington University in St. Louis, in the same *Newsweek* article. Finally, we may quote from a 1982 issue of the *Journal of the American Medical*

Association that underscores the therapeutic and prophylactic value of exercise: "There is no drug in current or prospective use that holds as much promise for sustained health as a lifetime program of regular exercise."

9

Eat for Life

"I realized when I retired that if I wanted a long life with quality, I needed to change my eating behavior and focus on the quality of foods."

"Nutrition is extremely confusing, and at my age why bother? After all these years, I'm unlikely to drastically change the foods I eat. If anything was going to happen to me, it would have by now."

The relevance of diet to wellness cannot be overstated. This most important aspect of our daily lives is influenced heavily by personal, family, and social factors. Nowhere is the element of choice more evident. The following questionnaire will preview some areas about nutrition in this chapter and show where you are already making healthy choices as well as where there may be room for improvement.

1. Which are myths and which are fact?
   (a) Asparagus, broccoli, and green beans are legumes.
   (b) Molasses, honey, and corn syrup are complex carbohydrates.
   (c) Only products of animal origin contain cholesterol.
   (d) Two 8-ounce glasses of skim milk meet the minimum adult daily requirements for calcium.

2. Putting on weight as I get older is all right because it's a natural process: the metabolic rate slows in most people as they age.
   True ( ) False ( )

3. Vitamin C has been in the news more than ever because research has shown that it and other antioxidant nutrients may protect against cancer and other diseases. Oranges and orange juice are by far the biggest source of vitamin C for Americans. Yet, ounce for ounce, which food has more vitamin C than oranges?
   (a) Broccoli
   (b) Red peppers
   (c) Strawberries
   (d) Kiwis
   (e) Red cabbage

4. Most people know that milk is an excellent source of calcium, but other foods are also rich in this essential mineral. Which of the following foods are?
   (a) Broccoli
   (b) Dried beans
   (c) Almonds
   (d) Dried figs

5. How many servings of fresh fruit and fresh vegetables should you eat per day? One serving is equal to one half cup.
   (a) 1
   (b) 2
   (c) 3
   (d) 4 or more

6. "Cholesterol free" and "fat free" are the same thing.
   True ( ) False ( )

7. Hydrogenated oils contain saturated fat.
   True ( ) False ( )

8. Which food is not a complex carbohydrate?
   (a) Rice
   (b) Apples
   (c) Apricots
   (d) Corn
   (e) Honey
   (f) Cereal
   (g) Bread

9. You can cut down on fat and cholesterol by eating more complex carbohydrates.
   True ( ) False ( )

10. Fruits are low in fat.
    True ( ) False ( )

Answers to the nutrition quiz:

Question 1:   (a), (b), and (d) are myths; (c) is fact.

Question 2:   (False) It is not all right because you'll probably live longer if you don't gain weight as you age. Slim, healthy people die at the slowest rates. According to the ongoing Framingham Heart Study,* people who weigh anywhere from 11 percent to 20 percent below the average weight for people of their height have the lowest risk of death.

Question 3:   (All) Brussels sprouts, green peppers, and arugula also have more vitamin C by weight than oranges.

Question 4:   (All) Ounce for ounce, all these foods contain as much or more calcium than milk. Of course, you shouldn't consume figs and almonds as your only source of calcium, since both are high in calories, and almonds are high in fat.

Question 5:   (d)

Question 6:   (False) Many oils are cholesterol-free but contain fat.

Question 7:   (True) The hydrogenation process adds saturated fat to otherwise healthy types of oil such as canola, soy, peanut, and olive oils.

Question 8:   Honey

Question 9:   (True) Eating pectin-rich fruits and legumes has been linked with lower blood cholesterol levels.

Question 10: (True) Except for avocados.

Visitors from abroad are struck by the rampant obesity of Americans and many complain of weight gain after they have been here a while.

---

*The Framingham, Massachusetts, study, begun in 1949, is a continuous project and is constantly being revised as new data are collected.

One woman from England told me she gained seven pounds in just five weeks after arriving in the United States.

In France, if you order a soft drink, you get a six-ounce bottle. In America, a "small drink" is easily a liter. In Spain, if you order a steak you get no more than eight ounces, but here a steak frequently is as large as the plate. Often instead of simple chocolate layer cake, one finds triple fudge cake with chocolate sauce, whipped cream, and nuts.

Many people today find it hard to locate food that's right for them and tastes good. Most folks would like to do the right thing, but are totally befuddled by the mixed messages received from magazines, radio, television, the federal government, advertisers, and friends. A blitz of nutrition advice in recent years tells you to lower your blood cholesterol level, eat more fiber, cut down on red meat, throw away salt shakers, decrease your fat intake, use olive oil, avoid barbecuing, watch out for shellfish, beware of hydrogenated fats, eat fewer eggs, check the lead level before drinking water from the tap, and so on. The mythology of nutrition is enormous. Eating is and should be a delight, but it should also be smart.

The U.S. rates of heart disease and some cancers, particularly those of the breast and colon, are among the highest in the world. Many factors, including an individual's genetic inheritance, contribute to cancer and heart disease, but when epidemiologists trace the course of diseases across the globe, the role of diet certainly stands out. For example, the traditional Japanese diet is the direct opposite of ours: typically rice, vegetables, and a little fish. By contrast many Americans put a big portion of meat in the center of the plate and add a few french fries. Consuming only about a quarter as much fat as we do, and far more carbohydrates, the Japanese live longer than anybody else in the world. That is, until they move here. "The Japanese in Japan have only one fifth the rate of breast cancer that we do," says Dr. Peter Greenwald, director of the Division of Cancer Prevention and Control at the National Cancer Institute. "When they move to Hawaii, the cancer goes up." In the last few years, moreover, as hamburgers, ice cream, and other high-fat foods have become popular in Japan, higher rates of cancer and heart disease have followed. Similar patterns are emerging all over the globe in those countries that imitate our diet.

The rates of disease are skyrocketing as they eat more animal fat and dairy products.*

Scientists now estimate that 40 percent of all cancer incidence in men, and 60 percent in women, is related to diet. The more fruits and vegetables people eat, the less likely they are to develop cancers of the colon, stomach, breast, and perhaps even of the lung. One reason may be that a plate crowded with vegetables can't hold as much of the fat that leads to colon and breast cancers, researchers say. Also, plants are loaded with fiber, which cuts the risk of colon cancer by evacuating harmful chemicals quickly from the body. Another reason is that vegetables such as broccoli, bok choy, turnips, kale, Brussels sprouts, cabbage, cauliflower, and collards (all known as the "cruciferous vegetables") contain nitrogen compounds called *indoles,* which appear to be effective against certain forms of cancer, particularly cancers of the stomach and large intestine.†

Most recent research has revealed other promising anti-cancer compounds in these vegetables. For example, cruciferous vegetables contain sulforphane, a compound that raises the activity of enzymes discouraging cancer growth. Some noncruciferous vegetables like carrots and green onions also contain sulforphane. Foods high in beta carotene such as carrots, sweet potatoes, winter squash, and dark green vegetables, all antioxidants, and vitamins C and E, help to sweep up cancer-promoting unstable oxygen molecules known as *free radicals.* The more intense a vegetable's green or yellow color, the more beta carotene it contains.

Adults in the United States need to do a better job of eating their fruits and vegetables, according to the national Nutrition Screening Initiative conducted jointly by the National Council on the Aging, the American Dietetic Association, and the American Academy of Family Physicians. Only 13 percent of adults between the ages of fifty-five and seventy-four eat the minimum recommended servings of fruits and vegetables daily. Between 15 and 20 percent of Americans over the age of sixty-five suffer from poor nutrition; 85 percent of older Americans

---

*See "Keeping Cancer at Bay with Diet," *The Johns Hopkins Medical Letter, Health After 50,* April 1994, and "Chemists Learn Why Vegetables Are Good for You," *New York Times,* April 13, 1993.

†University of California, *The Wellness Encyclopedia* (Boston: Houghton Mifflin, 1991).

have one or more chronic conditions that would benefit from nutrition intervention, and one in every four Americans is malnourished.

Everyone has to eat but it is astounding how few people are good at it. There seems to be a common dearth of dietary understanding: for example, how many calories a person should consume, how much fat and sodium is reasonable to eat, or what it means if a serving of cheddar cheese has 10 grams of fat. Many participants in my workshops entitled "Life Extension with Quality" fail the nutrition quiz at the beginning of the program (the one I presented at the outset of this chapter). Most answer incorrectly the following questions: "Are 'cholesterol free' and 'fat free' the same?" "Do hydrogenated oils contain saturated fat?" "Should a diet high in protein form the nucleus of your meals?" Says the Food and Drug Administration, "The public's understanding of nutrition remains relatively superficial." This is why there has been an overhaul in food labeling.

Many people are confused about what they are supposed to eat. Schools don't teach people very well and many consumers are so skeptical of nutritional claims that they have stopped trying to figure out what's good for them and what isn't. People get confused by the volume of data bombarding them in advertisements, television, breakfast cereal boxes, and stories told by friends.

It isn't always clear to the public at large which dietary guidelines are important or how to apply them on a day-to-day basis. It's strange that our society, with the greatest abundance of food, should leave understanding about the essentials of nutrition to chance or personal discovery, especially since nourishment is the foundation of health. Moreover, dieticians and scientists put nutrition information in language that many people do not understand. They talk, for example, about grams; but we're not on the metric system, so few people know what's being talked about when they read or hear the nutrition guidelines. Fortunately, under the new Nutrition Labeling Education Act passed by Congress in 1990, all packaged foods now have nutrition information designed to show shoppers how one food fits into an overall daily diet. The new labels help consumers follow more healthful diets and are reasonably easy to read.

What we consume and how we eat can influence how susceptible we are to carcinogens (cancer-causing substances), how well our bodies resist infections, our energy level, how well our hearts pump oxygen, whether we get diabetes, how we look and feel, and when we die.

The National Cancer Institute has reported that 80 percent of cancers are preventable and 35 percent of cancers are influenced by dietary factors. The United States Surgeon General's Report on Nutrition and Health has stated that poor diet contributes to two thirds of the deaths of the approximately 2.1 million Americans who die each year; many Americans not only eat too much food but they eat too much of the wrong foods; poor nutrition and lack of regular exercise have been strongly implicated in the development of the five big "killers": coronary heart disease, arteriosclerosis (hardening of the arteries), strokes, diabetes, and some types of cancer.

Many scientists and agencies, including the National Institutes of Health, realize that our focus ought to be preventing disease rather than trying to cure it, and that disease prevention begins with what people put in their mouths. A good idea would be to train primary care practitioners in nutrition, enabling them to counsel their patients in one of the most powerful of all preventive health practices—sound eating. This would be a good start to alleviating our dependence on the expensive medical system.

For most adult Americans, the ideal diet is low in fat and sodium (salt), moderate in protein, rich in calcium, and abundant in complex carbohydrates and fiber such as those found in whole grains, fruits, and vegetables. Fruits, grains, vegetables, and beans have little fat so they are always ideal choices.

Eating correctly is simple:

- Consume a minimum of five servings of vegetables and fruits daily, especially green and yellow vegetables and citrus fruits. A serving is equal to one half cup.

- Eat at least six servings each day of starches and complex carbohydrates such as breads, hot and cold cereals, legumes, rice, pasta, and potatoes.

- Consume no more than 6 ounces each day of high-protein foods like chicken, beef, pork, fish, and tofu, a quantity about the size of a deck of playing cards.

- Limit sodium intake to between 500 and 2400 milligrams each day, the equivalent of a bit more than one teaspoon of table salt.

- Keep your total fat intake at or below 30 percent of total calories consumed, and limit your intake of saturated fats (those from animal and dairy products), which contribute to high blood cholesterol, to 10 percent or less of total calories consumed. This 30 percent figure is recommended by the National Heart, Lung and Blood Institute as well as the American Heart Association and the American Cancer Society. Some health professionals say that total fat consumption should drop to 20 percent; more rigorous diets, such as those outlined by the Pritikin Longevity Center and by Dr. Dean Ornish, author of *Dr. Dean Ornish's Program for Reversing Heart Disease,* advise a limit of 10 percent. Dr. Ornish developed a study indicating that diet, exercise, and stress reduction can open clogged arteries and save lives.

Monitoring your fat intake is easy even though you may not be savvy about metric measurement. Simply count the grams of fat in your diet and when you have reached your limit, stop. How many grams of fat you should consume depends on your calorie needs. When you know that, it's just a matter of a simple calculation. For example, the average woman consumes about 1600 calories each day. To figure out the recommended amount of fat she can eat daily, simply drop the last zero in 1600 and divide by three, which equals 53 grams of fat. Inactive and active men burn about 2000 and 2500 calories daily, respectively, and can therefore eat 67 and 83 grams of fat, respectively. The new food labels will indicate how many grams of fat each serving contains.

The easiest way to make smart choices when food shopping or preparing a meal at home is to remember that fat, especially saturated fat found in animal and dairy products, is the biggest culprit in the American diet. If people know where the fat is and isn't, choices will be easier to make. Our culture is unique in that we have so many food choices: the average supermarket offers around 25,000 different items. It seems as if the consumer needs a Ph.D. in nutrition just to make an informed selection about which foods are the most healthy. Actually the new labeling on packaged foods makes choosing considerably easier than it used to be, so read these as well as the list of ingredients until you become familiar with those selections that are best for you. Reading the labels and lists of ingredients is important for everyone but it is especially helpful for those people who are regulating their diet in order to control or avoid problems such as heart disease, diabetes, hypertension, obesity, osteoporosis, kidney disease, and cancer. When purchasing processed foods, look at ingredient lists for hidden saturated fats in the form of tropical oils (coconut, palm, and palm kernel), hydrogenated vegetable oils (hydrogenation makes an oil more saturated), as well as cheese and butterfat.

You can begin with small modifications, because over time that will have a significant impact. Some people find that making small adjustments as they go along and learn is more palatable. Begin by examining your present eating patterns and identify where you need to make changes, then change the types of foods you eat and the quantity, if necessary. Write on a piece of paper what your goals are. Try not to do your regular food shopping when you are hungry because you may be less objective about your choices, and food shop when you have adequate time so you don't have to rush. Take your time to read those food labels carefully. In fact, read all the labels in the beginning because you'll probably be surprised at what you discover. Subscribe to one of the many excellent health magazines that are available today and shortly you'll find yourself teaching these important things about nutrition to your friends and family.

Remember your objective. Don't you want to live as long as possible with quality? Like that for exercise, the evidence of the benefit of sound eating practices is overwhelming. The foods you consume and your level of physical activity affect a number of risk factors involved in longevity. Also, diet and exercise are the elements of your health care over which you have the most control, and which do the most in influencing the risk of disease. When it comes to helping improve or maintain our health, our habits and choices can do much more than the entire medical establishment.

10

Check Up on Yourself

"I can do just about anything knowing I have my good health."

"I now realize how important health is. My decline in retirement has been chiefly due to my not taking care of myself."

Preventive health care is important. Ideally, we should do things that keep us healthy, such as exercising and eating carefully, as discussed in the previous chapters. Medical screenings are also vital but often overlooked. Even though we may have an "I feel great" attitude, we should consider medical screenings as another method to help us reach our objective of a quality long life.

If you answer "no" to any of the following questions, you need to reevaluate your alternatives by consulting with your physician.

1. Have you had your blood pressure checked in the past year?
   Yes ( ) No ( )

2. If you are over fifty, have you had a test for hidden blood in your stool within the last year?
   Yes ( ) No ( )

3. Do you know what your cholesterol level is?
   Yes ( ) No ( )

4. If you are a woman, do you examine your breasts for unusual changes or lumps at least once a month?
   Yes ( ) No ( )

5. If you are over fifty, have you had at least one endoscopic examination of your lower bowel?
   Yes ( ) No ( )

A fifty-six-year-old friend of mine was experiencing some discomfort. When it did not disappear after a few weeks, he reluctantly went to see a physician. The truth is, my friend's wife pleaded with him to go because it was not likely he would do so on his own. He hadn't been to a doctor in the past fifteen years except for a minor throat infection. After a doctor's appointment and some tests, the examination revealed nothing unusual: my friend was fine.

Another acquaintance of mine visited a physician following two months of symptoms. In this case, there was no phantom ailment; the examination and medical tests confirmed colon cancer, necessitating surgery. The physician told my friend that surgery probably could have been avoided had he had certain routine medical screening tests years before. Unfortunately, many people fail to realize that they have a problem until late in the course of an illness. As we age, many diseases do not manifest themselves with obvious symptoms. Changes in appetite, bowel habits, or sleeping patterns may provide subtle warnings that something is not quite right.

Today's astute consumer realizes that more medical tests don't necessarily translate into better health. A routine cluster of screening checks to detect diseases contributes little to positive health and usually increases medical costs dramatically, though a person's own situation and health history should determine the kinds and frequency of such tests.

Our focus needs to be on prevention. While many diseases, such as lung cancer, can be avoided through changes in lifestyle and environment, part of the risk of some diseases is beyond our control. We also know that risk increases with chronological age. Therefore, if you are over fifty, here are some tests that you should have done at regular intervals. These tests can perhaps uncover potential health problems before they interfere with your quality of life; such problems can best be treated if diagnosed early.

BLOOD PRESSURE

The American Heart Association estimates that more than 60 million adults in the United States—about one out of three—have high blood pressure, which increases the risk for heart disease, stroke, and kidney failure. You should have your blood pressure checked annually when visiting a doctor or nurse. Most high blood pressure, or hypertension, is identified before the patient reaches the age of fifty, but screening is so easy and inexpensive that it should be done routinely and periodically.

BLOOD CHOLESTEROL

High blood cholesterol is one of the major risk factors for coronary artery and heart disease and, as in high blood pressure, there are often no warning signs or symptoms. Fortunately, like high blood pressure, high blood cholesterol is reversible. A blood cholesterol test should be done every five years.

MAMMOGRAM

A mammogram is an X-ray of the breast and is one of the most valuable tools for the early detection of breast cancer. Mammograms show cancers too small to be felt during self examination. The earlier a lump is detected, the better a woman's chances are of being cured. According to the American Cancer Society, about 80 percent of breast cancers are noticed by women themselves during a breast self-examination or by simply noticing a lump. Nonetheless, many women discover breast lumps too late to benefit from any kind of treatment.

The best approach is to do a proper self-examination each month and combine it with a physician examination and mammogram annually after age fifty, once every one to two years between ages forty and forty-nine.

PAP SMEAR

Women have about a 1 percent chance of developing cervical cancer, which is treatable if caught early enough. The best way to detect the disease is to have a pap smear (a test introduced by the physician George Papanicolaou in 1943).

The American College of Obstetricians and Gynecologists advises women to have pap smears annually after they become sexually active; then, after they have had three consecutive normal smears, the test should be done every one to three years at the discretion of their doctor.

RECTAL EXAMINATION

For men over fifty, cancer of the prostate is the second leading cause of deaths due to cancer, after lung cancer. It affects about one of every eleven males. Early detection of prostate cancer allows the highest chance of cure, but, unfortunately, cancer confined to the prostate gland usually produces few symptoms. The American Cancer Society and the National Cancer Institute recommend as the most important tool in early detection a yearly digital rectal exam, which is simple, quick, and hardly deserving of the dread it seems to produce.

Recently a blood test to measure levels of the prostate-specific antigen—a protein produced in the prostate that may become elevated when cancer is present—has been under study. When this is combined with the conventional digital exam, the chances of detecting cancer appears to be greater than that of the digital exam alone.

Women should also have a rectal examination at the same time as a routine pelvic examination for detection of cancers of the colon and rectum.

FECAL OCCULT BLOOD TEST

Blood in the stool is one indicator of an abnormality in the colon, although it may be due to other, less serious causes, such as hemorrhoids. The occult blood test checks for minute traces of blood not detectable to the eye. Since the risk of bowel cancer increases significantly after fifty, early detection greatly increases the chances of a cure.

The test is easy to perform in the doctor's office or at home, and should be done annually after age fifty. Using a kit at home, the person obtains a series of stool samples, which are then treated chemically to determine if they contain hidden, or occult, blood.

SIGMOIDOSCOPY

Most experts agree that sigmoidoscopy, which is a visual examination of the lower part of the colon and the rectum using a thin, lighted tube, is the best method for early detection of tumors and precancerous growths of the colon and rectum. The American Cancer Society, the National Cancer Institute, and the American College of Physicians advise people to have a flexible sigmoidoscopic examination at ages fifty and fifty-one. If nothing is detected on either of these consecutive screenings, the exam should be repeated every five years.

If you are at high risk because of a family history of colon cancer, particularly if the disease was diagnosed when the relative was younger than fifty-five, then the first sigmoidoscopy should be done at age forty.

These tests are just one part of the medical picture. Your own physician will examine the results along with your past health history, your family history, and other tests he or she feels may be necessary.

The bottom line is that you must take care of yourself. Medical science will advance, but usually it will not be able to undo what you have already done to yourself. A healthy lifestyle must be your first priority.

11

Challenge the Mind and Renew the Spirit

"Retirement is life's renewal for doing those many things for which one thought there was never enough time."

"Don't become a do-nothing person like me."

What do retired people do all day? What do they do with the extra time not spent on essential tasks like food shopping, housework, and personal care? For preretirees engaged in an active and busy lifestyle, it can be difficult to imagine how to fill time after separating from work and a career.

After retired people complete the catchup activities—enjoying personal freedom, taking trips, reviving old friendships, cleaning the attic and garage, putting those pictures and slides of past vacations in chronological order, and playing golf or going fishing—many find their lives boring. "There is nothing new to do; nothing to provide a spark for my life" is a typical complaint. There are many possible reasons for this. Many people don't have postretirement alternatives, probably because they have been so focused on a single occupation for so many years. Others may require counseling and guidance to help alter a set of behaviors that keeps them from seeking out new possibilities. Still others may simply not have the required stamina because they have allowed themselves to deteriorate physically.

Our research shows that those retirees who participate in a variety of new and different activities tend to have more satisfying and fuller experiences. They simply seem to enjoy life more.

This chapter is for those people who enjoy doing interesting things and going to new places. Many of the suggestions are designed for or limited to people of a certain age whether retired or not. Other activities can be explored by adults of any age.

While certainly not exhaustive, the list that follows provides a tantalizing sampling of the many activities and opportunities available to help retired people repel tedium and lead active lives. It's a beginning: a selection of alternatives, an offering of travel ideas, projects, learning opportunities, events and associations. Some are "off the beaten path" and not often advertised, or easy to find.

People, of course, differ greatly in their individual tastes. An activity that interests and excites one retired person may have little or no appeal to another. Contained within this sampling should be something for everyone, providing at least a "springboard" for exploring the new and the different. Certainly, you should call or write for information about those that offer some appeal. Try a few. Get involved and have fun! They are first listed here by category and then described alphabetically in the following pages.

Nothing has more potential for adding meaning to life than the acquisition of new knowledge and experiences. It can turn retirement into a process of continuing growth and, of course, adventure.

HEALTH, FITNESS, AND SPORTS

Camp Rediscovery
Country Walkers
Elegant Ambles
National Senior Sports Association
Over the Hill Gang, International
Windjamming
Womanship

TRAVEL

Accommodations

Back to the Dorms
Chautauqua Institute
Education Exchange Club
Elderhostel
Evergreen Bed and Breakfast
Intervac
Vacation Exchange Club

Adventure

Golden Age Travellers Club
Outdoor Vacations for Women Over Forty
Outward Bound
Rainbow Adventures
Saga International Holidays
TravLtips
Vintage Air Tours

Handicapped

Flying Wheels Travel

Specialized

Grandtravel
Shelter Institute

SOCIAL

Good Sam Club
International Pen Friends
Merry Widows Dance Cruises
Solo Flights and Mature Tours

VOLUNTEERING

Earthwatch
Human Service Alliance
International Executive Service Corps
Literacy Volunteers of America
Meals on Wheels
National Forest Campground Host Program
Oceanic Society Expeditions
Peace Corps
Service Corps of Retired Executives Association (SCORE)
University Research Expeditions
Volunteers in Service to America (VISTA)

BACK TO THE DORMS

Fabulous Savings and Fabulous Holidays

More than seven hundred colleges and universities in the United States, Canada, and overseas open their campus dormitories and facilities for only $12 to $24 a day. These educational institutions rent out rooms to travelers offering secure, clean, and inexpensive lodgings. I am surprised to find many of the colleges and universities offering their facilities year round rather than just for the summer when I travel and take advantage of these bargains.

There are thirty-five centrally located universities in London, England, alone, with bed and breakfast at one-third the cost of regular lodging. Twenty-seven beautiful campuses up and down the state of California welcome you; forty-seven states, from Hawaii to Maine, as well as Washington, D.C., have delightful accommodations. In nearby Canada, eighty universities, stretching from the Atlantic to the Pacific, offer amazing overnight bargains. These facilities are not limited to students. Most of the campuses welcome families and adult travelers of all ages.

Nourishing, inexpensive meals with convenient transportation and accessible parking are usually available on most campuses. You'll discover at each location an atmosphere of friendliness that will enhance each day of your trip.

What to Expect When Staying in College Dorms

1. Clean, safe, comfortable sleeping quarters: double rooms with twin beds, although some colleges have suites, apartments, or single rooms.

2. Three varieties of bathrooms: private baths, attached baths connecting two rooms, and shared baths (showers and toilet down the hall).

3. Desks, chairs, closet space, television/lounge area, air conditioning, linen and travel service.

4. Access to sports facilities, the library, theater productions, workshops, food service, cultural events, parking, mail and telephone services.

Bring sleeping bags for children. Many colleges allow small children to sleep free in their parents' room. Some colleges offer cooking facilities. Cookware and utensils are useful if you intend to stay for an extended period. Bring tennis rackets, golf clubs, swim suits, and cameras.

To order a copy of the *U.S. and World Travel Accommodations Guide,* which lists the participating universities by state and country plus an assortment of travel tips, send $14.00 to:

Campus Travel Service
P.O. Box 5486
Fullerton, CA 92635

If you wish to call, the phone number is (800) 525-6633.

CAMP REDISCOVERY

Health, Fitness and Activities for Adults Over Fifty

Good health habits, physical activity, fun, and diet can vastly improve the quality of our lives, particularly as we get older. With this idea in mind, Camp Rediscovery was founded in 1984 to offer a unique health and fitness program specifically for adults fifty years old and over. Located in Palmyra, Virginia, Camp Rediscovery has 460 rolling acres of woodlands on the banks of the scenic Rivanna River, near Charlottesville.

The goal of the camp is to help campers gain a healthier lifestyle through a fun, stress-free experience. The informal atmosphere and highly trained, enthusiastic staff will make your stay exciting and enlightening.

Campers are free to choose their own activities: hiking, swimming, canoeing, archery, tennis, riflery, the rope course, fishing, aerobics, square dancing, horseback riding, and many others.

Unlike other health-oriented camps or resorts, Camp Rediscovery caters only to people fifty and over and allows participants to improve overall health, fitness, and health knowledge on an individual basis. The staff is handpicked from the best staffers of the University of Maryland's Adult Health and Development Program. They know that fitness and health should be fun!

A one-week session, with all meals and lodging included, is $325.00 per person. For more information write or phone:

Camp Rediscovery
2007 Pelden Road
Adelphi, MD 20783
(301) 405-2528

CHAUTAUQUA INSTITUTE

The Chautauqua Institute is an enchanting 856-acre hilltop Victorian village offering the best in fine and performing arts, education, religion, and recreation for people interested in enjoying themselves and improving their minds. Originally founded in 1874 as a summer tent colony for Sunday School teachers, this national historic landmark presents one of America's most notable summer festivals. Interestingly, almost every United States president has spoken there. For over one hundred years, Chautauqua has appealed to visitors of all ages and interests, but now includes a summer week and off-season weekends specifically for the over fifty-five crowd.

The institute's "55-Plus" weekends and "week in residence" for older adults are in their eighteenth year of operation. Programs focus on the arts, education, religion, and recreation. Each weekend presents a topic through discussion, workshops, lectures, films, cassette tapes, or any other appropriate means. Housing and meals are provided in a residence hall. The weekend begins on Friday afternoon and ends on Sunday for a cost of $105.

The "Residential Week for Older Adults" program is the last week of the nine-week Chautauqua Institute season, with all lectures and activities of the program. A moderate fee of $350 for the week provides

a gate ticket with admittance to most programs, including evening entertainment. Lodging and meals in a modern residence hall are included.

A week in September on "Experiencing the Arts" is an opportunity
for seniors to express their creativity.

The Chautauqua Institute is located in the southwestern corner
of New York State, halfway between Buffalo, New York, and Erie,
Pennsylvania. It is easy to reach by air or car and has been attracting
older people who like to create their own ideal vacations and something
very different.

For detailed program information and brochures write or call:

Ms. Judy Bloomquist
Coordinator
Program Center for Older Adults
Chautauqua, NY 14722
(716) 357-6310

COUNTRY WALKERS

Fine Walking and Hiking Vacations in Vermont and Maine

Country Walkers, Inc., has applied its thirteen years of knowledge and
experience to designing walks and hikes that offer an enlightening and
luxurious experience in some of the most beautiful natural areas of
northern New England, the Sonoran Desert in Arizona, the Olympic
Peninsula of Washington, and the South Island of New Zealand. More
than just an opportunity to exercise, these trips provide a close-up view
of the nature, culture, and people in these regions.

Trips cover between four and nine miles in a day, ranging in time
from three to five hours. Longer and shorter options are available for
the energetic or less active. Country Walkers excursions are not meant
to test your endurance, but to please your senses.

Group sizes are kept small. Two- and three-day trips are limited
to between eighteen to twenty participants and five-day trips to eighteen
people. Smaller groups naturally form by themselves during the outing,
allowing people the flexibility to walk at their own pace and stop as
often as desired.

Inns are chosen for their graciousness, superior food and accommodations, and quiet and scenic locations.

Country Walkers' exceptional guides include naturalists, historians, and professional wildlife photographers, all of whom help provide an enlightening experience. Each trip is designed to highlight the special features of a region and season. Whether it's a magnificent sunrise walk on Cadillac Mountain, in Maine's Acadia National Park, kicking up your heels at a local square dance, or an evening of summer theater, the culture and natural beauty of these areas remain a memorable part of the trip.

For detailed information, write to or call:

Country Walkers, Inc.
P.O. Box 180-NC
Waterbury, VT 05676-9742
(802) 244-1387

EARTHWATCH

Adventure, Fellowship, Challenge, and Growth

If you're willing to travel to unusual places throughout the United States and abroad, to meet fascinating new people of all ages and nationalities, to open your mind to new perspectives and ideas, and in the process to help make this planet a better place for everyone, Earthwatch may be the opportunity for you.

Earthwatch is a nonprofit organization that works a little like the Peace Corps. It organizes expeditions to research sites worldwide for leading scholars and scientists, and then recruits men and women who are interested in serving as staff volunteers. For example, an Argentinean archaeologist needs volunteers to help locate the settlement upon which Buenos Aires grew; an Australian ecologist needs help collecting data on Kangaroo Island's plants; a Montana paleontologist is trying to determine why dinosaurs were still on the prowl half a million years after they had been supposedly destroyed by a falling asteroid. Staff volunteers may spend a summer odyssey in the Gulf of Alaska to help record weather patterns from ocean vessels that can judge how often you'll need to carry your umbrella once you get home; or they may assist in researching volcanoes in Costa Rica.

Since its founding in 1971, Earthwatch has provided a meeting ground for people seeking worthwhile outlets for their interests and skills. Members include retired couples, graduate students, singles, lawyers, carpenters, teachers, doctors, artists, architects, mechanics, and others looking to contribute to the betterment of the world. Earthwatch has mobilized and staffed over one thousand projects in eighty-three countries—preserving the world's endangered habitats and species, exploring the vast heritage of people, and promoting health and international cooperation.

Members are also invited to special outings, lectures, and receptions in their area so they can meet scholars, scientists, authors, and fellow members.

Expeditions are listed in each issue of *Earthwatch* magazine and members can select the one that best suits their schedule, interests, and budget. Members can volunteer for as many days as they care to give. Expedition costs are kept at a minimum by sharing with other team members and are 100 percent tax deductible. Members stay in inexpensive hostels, dormitories, private homes, and campgrounds; eat local cuisines; and enjoy local customs and cultural experiences.

For further information, write or call:

Earthwatch
680 Mt. Auburn Street
Box 403
Watertown, MA 02272
(800) 776-0188

ELDERHOSTEL

For Learning and Adventure

A lifetime of experience and an inquiring mind are all you need to enjoy the Elderhostel experience of your choice. Nearly two hundred thousand individuals participate each year.

Elderhostel is a program combining education with travel, culture, and recreation specifically for Americans age sixty years and older.* It is committed to the belief that retirement does not represent an end to significant activity for older adults but a new beginning filled with opportunities, challenges, and adventures.

---

*A spouse fifty years old or older may accompany a participant who is at least sixty years of age.

The word "hostel" traditionally implies simple accommodations at a modest cost. Participants enjoy inexpensive, short-term academic programs at educational institutions around the world. Students live on the campus of their host institutions while attending a program and have access to the cultural and recreational facilities and resources there.

Elderhostel has its origins in the youth hostels of Europe and the folk schools of Scandinavia,* where residential settings had a positive impact on adult education programs offered by the folk high schools. Introduced in 1975 on five university campuses in New Hampshire, Elderhostel has grown to more than 1,700 educational programs offered in all fifty states, all ten Canadian provinces, and over forty-two countries.

This probably is one of the best educational travel bargains available. With over 1,600 universities, colleges, museums, state and national parks, environmental education centers, conference centers, and other educational and cultural institutions throughout the United States and abroad participating, Elderhostel can provide low-cost accommodations and a limitless variety of programs.

Elderhostel programs are in the liberal arts and sciences. Each institution selects the courses it wishes to offer; the result is an intellectual smorgasbord of impressive proportions. Anyone can find a program with courses to his or her liking—it would be difficult not to. Courses are not for credit and there are no examinations, grades, or, except for the Intensive Studies program, required homework. The programs presuppose no particular knowledge or study. The educational background of participants can range from high school dropouts to Ph.Ds.

Elderhostel is a wonderful way to exchange ideas, sample college life, and make new friends with active, interesting people. It is a unique opportunity to combine study with the adventure of exploring new places in a friendly and supportive academic environment.

The average Elderhostel tuition is $350 for a one-week program in the United States. This fee covers lodging, meals, all classes, and a variety of extracurricular activities. It also covers any course-related field trips that may be offered. International programs are two to four weeks in length with comparable tuition costs. Scholarships are available to people who require financial assistance to attend. Information about scholarships can be found in Elderhostel's catalogs.

---

*These were classrooms in which village elders served as teachers.

As one person wrote, "I've been to fifty-one Elderhostels, and there has never been one that didn't offer me something good. I have met people who never finished grammar school, and some with as many as five advanced degrees. White, black, brown, red, and yellow . . . blue collar, white collar, and no collar at all. At Elderhostel you meet *people.*"

The following is a small sampling of course titles from the nearly two thousand offered that represent the interesting and unusual as well as the traditional: Watersheds and Wilderness; The Wild Ways of Plants; Nineteenth-Century Italian Opera; Ragtime; Let's Look at Antiques; Shakespeare's Women; Is Anyone Out There?; The Scablands Habitat; Clean and Decent: A History of Baths; Oceanography; Seizing Control of Your Health: Preventive Medicine; World War II: Battlefields and the Home Front; Wildflowers in Diverse Habitats; Agatha Christie: "Weaving the Web of Suspense"; Chinese Culture and Travel; Beginning Genealogy Workshop; Your Lifestyle and Your Heart; Exploring the Smokies with Your Grandchildren; Wines of the World; King Arthur—Fact or Fiction?; Growing During the Adult Years; The Amazing Arthropods; How to Be a Good Tourist; Ghost Towns of Eastern Oregon; The Roaring Twenties: A Decade of Diversity; The Mystery of Glass; Backstage Broadway; Using Both Sides of Your Brain; Introduction to Drawing; Astronomical Frontiers; The Crash of 1987; Outdoor Photography; Bugs! Bats! and What's That?; Mummies of Ancient Egypt; The Honorable Art of Clowning; Better Writing for Fun and Profit; Organic Gardening; The Plucked Dulcimer; Stained Glass; and Dinosaur Tracks, Petroglyphs, and Pioneer Relics.

For information and a free copy of the current catalog, write to or call:

Elderhostel
75 Federal Street
Boston, MA 02110
(617) 426-7788

ELEGANT AMBLES

International Walking Holidays

Elegant Ambles personally designs, arranges, and conducts exhilarating yet relaxing walking tours into the coziest corners of the world. It most frequently receives requests for private tours to Great Britain, Switzerland, Japan, New England, and California, but it can assist with travels anywhere.

The Secret

The secret of vacation enjoyment is simple. Elegant Ambles selects those marvelously delightful, yet little-known destinations far removed from the typical tourist crowds. Then, in conjunction with private or public transportation, a small group radiates out on daily guided walks, all comfortably suited to each participant's own choice of length and pace.

Travel Style

Elegant Ambles offers a unique combination of the healthy delights of walking with the appealing pleasures of distinctive accommodations. You can choose from "bed and breakfast" style with bath down the hall to romantic country inns to legendary castles replete with royal feasts. Each refreshing journey is normally two to three weeks long with three to seven unhurried days spent in each charming place.

Trip Highlights

These remarkable odysseys introduce travelers to fascinating cultures, tantalizing cuisines, and breathtaking countrysides. Participants discover remote realms and tucked-away treasures. They travel along farmer's footpaths, through cobblestone villages, past serene lakeside cafes and around spectacular alpine outposts. The result is a total immersion in both sensational scenic wonders and colorful village life.

The Services

The expertise of Elegant Ambles in travel planning covers three areas:

1. Custom-designed tours for private parties of all ages, typically with one to eight participants, plus an experienced tour leader. Prices vary from $95 to $295 per person per day, depending upon the style of travel desired.

2. Individualized travel consulting services, including detailed itinerary design, for those who enjoy independent travel without a personal guide. Rates reflect services requested.

3. Helping people join privately organized tours. Some of these groups welcome extra people on their tour and are happy to inform interested travelers about these special openings.

If this approach to travel appeals to you, you may obtain further information by writing or calling:

Elegant Ambles
Box 6616
San Diego, CA 92106-0616
(619) 222-2224

EVERGREEN BED AND BREAKFAST

For Singles or Couples over Fifty

This is a unique organization founded over ten years ago to provide unusual travel accommodation savings by using already existing hospitality resources—those spare guest rooms that so many people over fifty have now that their children have grown and left home. No matter how exquisite or simple a home is, or how near or how far from the beaten path, people who have guest rooms to let can make them available to fellow club members. Annual membership in the organization costs $50 per couple or $40 for singles. Members receive an annual directory, a membership card, and a quarterly newsletter. Participants can enjoy comfortable sleeping accommodations and a wholesome breakfast in the private home of a member host. The moderate gratuity, payable to the host, is under $25 and includes breakfast. The same gratuity applies regardless of where a member stays. There are five hundred host locations throughout the United States.

Based on information supplied in the host directory, members arrange their accommodations by contacting their hosts directly. Visits may be arranged for up to three days, depending upon availability. Members can realize some big savings while traveling and can meet some fascinating people along the way.

Once you know where you plan to go, and when, you review your membership directory to find members located in the area you plan to visit. Then you contact them to see whether you can stay with them on the dates you have chosen.

As a traveler, the Evergreen Club will open up many delightful opportunities to meet interesting people. As a host, you'll have a chance to return some of the hospitality that has been extended to you. Don't expect large numbers of guests flocking to your door. Few members are called upon to serve as hosts more than three to four times a year, so your guest room isn't apt to get worn ragged. At the same time, you can travel as often as you want without any sense that you are imposing on others.

For more information call or write:

Evergreen/Travel Club
404 N. Galena Avenue
Dixon, IL 61021
(815) 288-9600

FLYING WHEELS TRAVEL

Travel for the Handicapped

Flying Wheels Travel, Inc., founded in 1970, arranges group tours and independent travel for the physically handicapped and their friends and relatives. A pioneer in the development of travel for the physically handicapped to make their trips a more enjoyable, comfortable adventure, the organization's primary concerns are quality and personal care. The specialized facilities that it provides are geared toward individuals rather than groups.

Each tour is planned with the disabled traveler in mind, whether it is a group-planned tour or a completely independent itinerary. Just let Flying Wheels Travel know where and when you want to go and they will make all the necessary arrangements. All you need to do is to submit in writing:

1. A basic idea of the itinerary you wish to follow
2. The length of time you intend to be gone
3. Any major points of interest you want to include
4. Requirements for accessibility
5. An estimated budget.

Flying Wheels will then go through the itinerary to determine accessibility and make modifications and suggestions, if necessary, to arrive at your final program. The organization does not charge for its services; however, a $50 "Goodwill Deposit" is requested. This deposit is then fully credited toward the final billings for airline transportation, hotel accommodations, and the like.

For information and a brochure, call or write to:

Flying Wheels Travel, Inc.
143 West Bridge
P.O. Box 382
Owatonna, MN 55060
(800) 535-6790

GOLDEN AGE TRAVELLERS CLUB

The Golden Age Travellers Club was founded in 1969 with a purpose of providing great bargains on social and travel events for people over fifty years of age. The membership consists of over 8,000 active individuals and it offers a wide selection of cruises, tours, and rail and sail programs.

Most of the trips are cruises to the Mediterranean, China, Japan, the South Pacific, New England, Canada, the Mexican coast, the Panama Canal, the Caribbean, Alaska, Catalina Island, Russia, Hawaii, and many other places. Some gala cruises offer 40 to 50 percent off the brochure rate. Golden Age Travellers Club also offers Land Holidays to Spain, Portugal, Costa Rica, and Guatemala from one to three weeks at discounted rates.

Membership is $10 a year for singles and $15 for couples, which includes a variety of benefits such as a quarterly travel digest, discounts and/or bonuses on major cruise lines ranging from 5 percent to 50 percent off the regular published tariff rates, a credit of $15 to $25 per person against the transportation costs to the airport on certain trips, an incentive bonus point program against future trips, and early booking discounts. Single travelers can enroll in the "Roommates Wanted" list to help find a companion to share costs.

To receive a free information package, call or write to:

Golden Age Travellers
Pier 27, Port of San Francisco
The Embacadero
San Francisco, CA 94111
(800) 258-8880

THE GOOD SAM CLUB

This is an international organization of recreational vehicle (RV) users that provides a number of valuable and interesting benefits.

Since most people in trailers and motorhomes are over fifty years old, this organization can certainly be of assistance when traveling the country. The most important option is the Good Sam emergency road service and towing regardless of vehicle size, because most automobile clubs do not provide RV service or towing. The few that do offer only minimal coverage. The Good Sam Emergency Road Service includes the RV and other vehicles as well.

Other benefits are 10 percent discounts on fees at thousands of parks and campgrounds as well as discounts on RV parts and accessories at major RV service centers. Propane gas is also discounted. Other membership services include:

- Lost pet service
- Lost key service
- Credit card protection
- RV financing
- Travelers checks
- Mail forwarding
- Trip routing
- Bank card service and rebates
- The club magazine
- Caravan gatherings—"samborees"
- Campground directories
- Vehicle insurance
- Group medical, hospital, and life insurance

Membership costs $19 a year per family.
For free information and brochures call or write to:

The Good Sam Club
P.O. Box 6888
Englewood, CO 80155
(800) 234-3450

GRANDTRAVEL

Very Special Vacations for Grandparents and Grandchildren

Developed by a team of teachers, psychologists, and leisure counselors, Grandtravel is dedicated to helping grandparents create lasting memories for themselves and their grandchildren.

Today's grandparents live more active and independent lives than did their grandparents. However, great distances may prevent them from seeing their children and grandchildren as often as they would like. The nuclear family is often scattered today, and people are constantly seeking ways to draw their family closer together. Years of experience as parents have taught grandparents how important support, nurturing, and affection are to their relationships with their grandchildren.

Grandtravel is a vacation travel program designed for grandparents and grandchildren who wish to share the pleasures of traveling together. It's ideal for grandfathers, grandmothers, grandchildren, and almost anyone else, such as aunts, uncles, or friends who wish to travel with a child. Children of any age are welcome, but experience has shown that those between the ages of seven and seventeen especially enjoy the trips.

Grandtravel is a carefully researched travel concept that gives special attention to the benefits that come from intergenerational experiences. Tours go just about anywhere in the world and are selected with school curricula in mind to enhance the education of the young travelers. Grandtravel escorts tell them about an area's history and heritage, its people and culture. New destinations are constantly being added to the program, many at the request of the grandtravelers themselves.

The tours are escorted from departure to return: Grandtravel escorts are teachers or leisure counselors responsible for the academic component of the tour as well as for cultural activities and games. Escorts also assist tour guides with tour interpretations for grandchildren.

Deluxe, first-class, or best-available hotels near attractions and recreation facilities are selected for the trips. Meals that are balanced as well as delicious are provided on a fixed schedule, with both traditional and local foods being offered. Between points of interest, travelers ride in comfortable air-conditioned motorcoaches.

To preserve the special memories of their trip, all grandtravelers will receive a photo album and travel diary.

For more detailed information and a brochure, please call or write:

Grandtravel
6900 Wisconsin Avenue
Suite 706
Chevy Chase, MD 20815
(800) 247-7651

HUMAN SERVICE ALLIANCE

Opportunities to Grow While Serving Others

Are you interested in working with a dedicated team that shares a common vision of serving others? Have you ever thought of taking a "service vacation"?

Human Service Alliance (HSA) is a nonprofit organization whose purpose is to foster the ideal of serving humanity selflessly, in the spirit of love and joy. It represents an idea that ordinary human beings, with jobs and families, can do extraordinary things when they choose to work together as a group to serve others. HSA is composed completely of volunteers—there is no paid staff and all of its services are provided free of charge. This service takes many forms: care for the terminally ill, education and respite care for families with a developmentally disabled child, enhancement of health and wellness, and mediation opportunities for people with disputes to come together and cooperatively work out solutions.

HSA is also a working model for those interested in learning how to run an organization of this kind. Located in Winston-Salem, North Carolina, HSA has attracted worldwide recognition and participation. In 1991, President George Bush recognized the organization as a "Point of Light," and the Sara Lee Foundation awarded HSA with one of its four National Leadership Awards for excellence. In 1993, HSA was selected internationally as one of thirteen nonprofit finalists to be featured in a series of thirty-minute television documentaries called "The Visionaries."

At HSA, volunteers come together in a setting of group work and have the opportunity to serve in the Center for the Care of the Terminally Ill. Excellent training and supervision is provided to all who volunteer. One role is to care directly for the guests, much as a loving family member would: keeping them company, reading to them, or simply holding hands. In addition to direct care, there are other equally important functions, including cooking, housekeeping, gardening and grounds maintenance, carpentry, general building maintenance, typing, computer work, and other activities. There are opportunities for everyone—all ages and backgrounds.

There are comfortable rooms available for full-time, live-in volunteers in the new eight-thousand-square-foot building where the center is located. Meals are also provided so that full-time volunteers incur minimal living expenses. Basic medical services are also provided. People from all over the world volunteer at HSA, staying for varying periods of time—some for a few months, a year, and even longer.

If you are interested in participating, call or write to:

Human Service Alliance
3983 Old Greensboro Road
Winston-Salem, NC 27101
(910) 761-8745

INTERNATIONAL EXECUTIVE SERVICE CORPS

Among our country's little-known but great resources are the thousands of retired American men and women business executives, public administration officials, and academicians who have volunteered their experience and skills to stimulate the economies of countries all over the world.

International Executive Service Corps (IESC) was established by a group of American businessmen and women in 1964 for the transfer of managerial and technical expertise to less developed countries. It was formally announced by President Lyndon Johnson in ceremonies in the White House Rose Garden on June 15, 1964. Presently, IESC has offices in fifty countries, each headed by a resident director of operations.

The transfer of technology and managerial expertise has been achieved by volunteers through IESC's partnership of business and government. IESC is unique in that it operates on a global scale, yet remains very personal. It is not a government-to-government program but a people-to-people activity. In assisting almost every kind of enterprise known to the business and institutional world, IESC has generated growth, created jobs, instilled confidence, sold U.S. products, and left behind significant goodwill.

IESC helps developing countries grow, take care of themselves, and become better customers of the United States. With the support of its principal sponsor, the United States government's Agency for International Development, IESC's program activity includes:

- Seeking environmental solutions
- Privatizing state-owned enterprises
- Building economic participation of women
- Economic reform and institution building
- Increased small and microenterprise development.

IESC has the largest private executive skill bank of industry-specific knowledge in the world, and it has shared these skills in fifteen thousand projects in more than one hundred countries. People with backgrounds in the corporate world and agribusiness, hotel operation, restaurants, health, the judiciary, government, education, banking and investing, and many other fields are welcome to participate.

Most volunteers are retirees though many others not yet retired use their vacation or company leave time to complete projects. There are no age restrictions because IESC believes you are only as old as you feel. Some volunteers are in their eighties, yet they are well on top of skills in their field, have a spirit of adventure, and want to help others.

For more information and a detailed brochure, call or write to:

IESC
P.O. Box 10005
Stamford, CT 06904-2005
(800) 243-4372
(203) 967-6000

INTERNATIONAL PEN FRIENDS

"The Sun Never Sets on IPF"

Have you ever considered that the greatest friend you may ever have is someone you have never met, living in a land you have never seen? International Pen Friends (IPF) can provide you with new friends in your own age group in many places. This organization has over 300,000 members in 188 countries and is regarded as the greatest pen friend club in the world. It has helped promote goodwill and friendship on an international scale.

IPF is open to the young and the mature, male and female, married and single. The youngest member is eight years old and the oldest is over a hundred. The club includes people, many of them retired, from all walks of life: past and present military personnel, artists, bankers, business people, clergy, computer programmers, dancers, doctors, engineers, social workers, scientists, secretaries, students, teachers, and many others.

Whether you are interested in cultivating congenial friendships, practicing a foreign language, improving your technical knowledge, arranging exchange holidays, or developing your hobbies, you can choose from among 300,000 members to find new, exciting, and interesting contacts. For example, IPF has its own Stamp Exchange Division with over 5,000 members.

Founded in Dublin, Ireland, in 1967, IPF employs over five hundred club agents worldwide and utilizes five computers and five printers to provide service. The club literature is available in the following languages: English, Danish, French, German, Italian, Lithuanian, Portuguese, Russian, and Spanish.

The club also publishes its own international magazine, *People & Places.* Members are encouraged to submit articles and photographs for publication.

For those aged twenty-one to sixty the annual single membership is $18 and double membership is $24. Those over sixty years of age pay $15 per year.

For more information, call or write to:

International Pen Friends
Leslie Fox, Regional Representative
P.O. Box 65
Homecrest Station
Brooklyn, NY 11229
(718) 769-1785

INTERVAC—U.S.

The Largest Home Exchange Network in the World

Many have heard about it—more and more are doing it. Singles, couples, and families living in exciting places in the United States and around the world are trading their homes and experiencing the kind of vacation that most people only dream about. "Exchangers" vacations are spent in the comfort of a private home located in the city or town in which the travelers are visiting. The savings and convenience of home exchanging have enabled people to vacation in places they might otherwise never be able to afford.

Home exchanging has many advantages. No hotel tab at vacation's end has an obvious appeal. Savings continue with cooking meals "at home," shopping in neighborhood stores, and using the exchange partner's car, which eliminates costly automobile rental. Feeling like a resident instead of a tourist is an important asset, and knowing that home, pets, and plants will be taken care of adds the intangible factor of freedom from worry. Home exchanging eases the problems of traveling with children and lessens the strain of living out of a suitcase. You can experience an environment totally different from your own, whether it is in the United States or abroad, and reap educational rewards not found in any book.

Whether you live in a city apartment, a suburban home, a seaside resort, or on a farm in the country, there are people like you who are as eager to experience the environment and culture you call "home" as you are to experience theirs.

Founded in 1953, Intervac offers to its subscribers over seven thousand exchange opportunities yearly in more than thirty-five countries. For more information and a free brochure, call or write to:

Intervac
P.O. Box 590504
San Francisco, CA 94159
(800) 756-HOME
(415) 435-3497

LITERACY VOLUNTEERS OF AMERICA

Enabling Adult Nonreaders to Achieve Personal Goals through Literacy

The national statistics are staggering: adult illiteracy is creating an enormous economic drain, affecting every type and size of business. In September 1993, the most detailed portrait ever available on the condition of literacy in this nation was released by the U.S. Department of Education. It showed that 23 percent of adults, about 44 million, are functionally illiterate. (Functional illiteracy refers to an individual's inability to use reading, speaking, writing, and computational skills in everyday life situations. The functionally illiterate person is unable to fill out an employment application, follow written instructions, or read a newspaper.) Another part of the survey showed that about 28 percent— fifty million adults—were at the second-lowest level. These individuals are marginally literate and their everyday skills still quite limited.

Literacy Volunteers of America, Inc. (LVA), is a national, nonprofit organization combatting illiteracy through a network of 455 active community programs in forty-four states. LVA provides tutoring and other educational services directly to persons desiring increased literacy skills, including English as a second language. The volunteers, supported by professional staff, serve as tutors, tutor trainees, secretaries, administrators, planners, communicators, and in other functions necessary to achieve the mission of universal adult literacy.

LVA was founded in Syracuse, New York, in 1962; by the end of 1993 it consisted of about 43,000 volunteers, many of them retired, serving 50,000 learners. If you enjoy reading and like to help people, you can be a Literacy Volunteer. The organization will train you and match you with an adult who needs help. Or, if you do not want to tutor, you may volunteer as an office worker, a program manager, a fundraiser, or for a variety of other jobs.

To locate the adult literacy program nearest you, you may ask for information at your local library, consult your local phone directory for a listing under "Literacy," or call the National Literacy Hotline: (800) 228-8813. This office links callers with literacy programs in their areas. Individuals receive a literacy referral on the telephone and a followup information packet in the mail.

You may also write to:

Literacy Volunteers of America, Inc.
Field Services Department, Box 1
5795 Widewaters Parkway
Syracuse, NY 13214

MEALS ON WHEELS

Meals on Wheels was developed after a survey by the National Council on Aging revealed that many older persons are unable either to get out to do adequate marketing or to prepare a proper, nutritious meal. Surveys show that one-third of noninstitutionalized Americans over sixty-five live alone. Thirty percent skip meals almost daily and 25 percent have incomes under $10,000. Forty-five percent take multiple prescription medications. Each of these factors can signal a person at risk for poor nutrition.

The Meals on Wheels service is usually sponsored by a public or a nonprofit organization. The law requires that the meals must meet one-third of the daily recommended food requirement and menus must be approved by the state nutritionist. Volunteers deliver the meals; since each volunteer has only a few stops, the food can be delivered hot at mealtime.

This program is available to any older person who is physically disabled and confined to his or her home, either on a permanent or temporary basis. Charges are based on the individual's ability to pay and are quite modest. Some needy older persons don't pay anything.

Your local senior center or Area Agency on Aging (which can be found in the government section of the telephone directory) can give you information if a Meals on Wheels program or Senior Nutrition Program is operating in your community.

MERRY WIDOWS DANCE CRUISES

"Get Out Your Dancing Shoes and Get Ready for Fun!"

No more sitting on the sidelines while other cruise passengers are out on the dance floor! A Merry Widow Dance Cruise gives ladies sun-filled days and fun-filled nights with professional dance partners to keep them whirling around the dance floor.

The Merry Widows is a group of single, widowed, and divorced ladies who like to dance but don't have partners. A lady's dancing skill is not an issue as long as she is willing to have fun. Most ladies on the Merry Widows Dance Cruises are thirty to ninety years of age; they may have had a number of dance lessons or may not have danced in twenty years.

Merry Widows dance partners are selected from professional dance studios across the country. Not only are they excellent dancers, but they are also good conversationalists and charming companions. Dance cards are provided with the lady's partners' names listed for each night of dancing, and partners are rotated. A professional dancer is provided for every five ladies, allowing free time for them to relax and freshen up. The dancers are not paid for their services, nor do they accept tips. The ladies also dine with these gentlemen, who range in age from thirty-five to sixty-five.

Approximately four times a year, the Merry Widows sail on some of the finest ships afloat. Destinations and length of the cruises vary from a seven-day sail on the Caribbean, to ten days in Canada and New England, to a sixteen-day exotic adventure in the Orient.

The Merry Widows Dance Cruises is an original concept by Phyllis W. Zeno, who organized this program in 1977, and satisfied repeat passengers attest to the success of the concept. The cruises are structured to provide complete freedom and enjoyment without any pressure or embarrassment.

Here are testimonials from a few of the ladies: "It just gets better and better! I was on the first Merry Widow Dance Cruise in 1977, and I've been on fifteen more since. I can hardly wait til the next one!" "My first trip as a single. I found it very enjoyable. Using a scale of 1 to 10, I would rate the dance hosts a 10." "This was one of the best vacations I ever had. The food, entertainment, and facilities were excellent, and having the men to dance with each night was wonderful. They were a group of great guys."

For more information, call or write to:

> Merry Widows Dance Cruises
> P.O. Box 31087
> Tampa, FL 33631
> (813) 289-5923

NATIONAL FOREST CAMPGROUND HOST PROGRAM

A Forest Service Campground Host is a volunteer who agrees to spend part or all of the camping season in a national forest campground. The program offers an opportunity to join and become involved with the Forest Service, the agency responsible for promoting conservation and wise use of forest land in the United States. Almost anyone who wants to become involved may apply, and such assets as a sense of humor, patience, and the willingness and ability to work well with the public are important. Retired people make particularly fine campground hosts.

A campground host is always provided with a free campsite; many of these sites have full hookups for a recreational vehicle. Some districts even provide some type of housing for their volunteers, ranging from dorm-type housing to travel trailers and even larger mobile homes or cabins. A stipend or reimbursement for incidental expenses is often provided.

The job for a host varies in each district but the main function is to make other campers feel welcome and at home. In addition to information about the campground, hiking trails, and areas of interest, hosts are also asked many other questions. Campers may want to know, for example, where to purchase ice, gasoline, propane, groceries, and souvenirs, as well as the location of churches, doctors, hospitals, telephones, and laundromats.

Hosts may stay at each campground for as long as they wish during the camping season from Memorial Day through Labor Day. Some stay for two weeks, a month, or the entire season.

The campground host is the most important link between the campers and the Forest Service, whose personnel go home in the evenings and have days off. Without hosts, they would have no idea what goes on at the campground when they aren't there.

Seasoned hosts report that their work is one of the most wonderful experiences they have ever had. They haven't yet volunteered for any place that they would not consider returning to again. And they make many, often permanent new friendships in every campground. Hosts also say that they are never bored. "Bored is one thing we have never been. Other people, and our work, see to that."

For more general information about the National Forest Campground Host Program, call (618) 833-8576, or if you are interested in volunteering at a particular campground, contact the district office and they will be able to provide you with details. If you are not familiar with the different national forests (there are 156), request a copy of "A Guide to Your National Forests" from any National Forest Service office or call or write to:

> U.S. Forest Service—Publications
> 201 14th Street SW
> Washington, D.C. 20250
> (202) 205-0957

NATIONAL SENIOR SPORTS ASSOCIATION

For Older Americans Who Enjoy Travel, Sports, and New Friendships

The National Senior Sports Association (NSSA) is a growing fellowship of men and women fifty years of age or older who want to maintain and improve their physical and emotional health through sports participation. NSSA is a national organization dedicated to helping members experience a sporting good life.

The NSSA organizes and conducts recreational and competitive tournaments in golf, tennis, and bowling at resorts you've always wanted to visit. Using group purchasing power and off-season scheduling, NSSA offers extremely attractive package plans that enable members to fulfill their dreams of sports-oriented travel and enjoy the fun and fellowship of friendly competition or recreational play.

Many members are in their sixties, seventies, and eighties. While most members are married couples, others are single or widowed. Some have found that a common interest in a favorite sport leads to an awareness of other common experiences and joys. The NSSA has had many marriages within the fellowship.

With participants grouped by skill level, those who want competition find it. Those who simply wish to enjoy friendly recreational play, even beginners, may do so. There are no "sports widows or widowers" at NSSA outings. For those who don't participate in the sports, there is always a special program of tours to local attractions, shopping excursions, and other activities that can be enjoyed while a spouse is busy on the courses, courts, or lanes.

Membership is $25 for one year and $65 for three years. A lifetime membership is $150. Once they join, members receive a monthly membership newsletter, with articles describing upcoming outings, and an enrollment form. They are also eligible for many other benefits, such as discounts at major car rental companies, discounts on some sports equipment and apparel, air travel assistance, awards and prizes, and the NSSA Gold Mastercard.

For additional information and a package of materials, call or write to:

> National Senior Sports Association, Inc.
> 1248 Post Road
> Fairfield, CT 06430
> (800) 282-6772

OCEANIC SOCIETY EXPEDITIONS

Oceanic Society Expeditions is a nonprofit organization founded in 1972 to create opportunities for individuals to learn about the natural world through participation in educational ecotours and research expeditions. There has been a growing appreciation of the importance of biological diversity to the health of our planet. Oceanic Society Expeditions believes that responsibly conducted nature tourism can help save natural areas by contributing to the "business" of conservation.

Oceanic Society Expeditions conducts ecotours with a noninvasive approach to viewing wildlife and wilderness exploration. Most of the trips offered are "soft adventures"; that is, they are not rugged, and are accessible to people with a broad range of lifestyles. Thousands of people of all ages and backgrounds have traveled with this organization. Participants may travel alone, with a friend, or as a family.

Although Oceanic Society Expeditions travels to areas off the beaten path, no special skills or experiences are needed. The trips are designed to be enjoyed by anyone in general good health. All itineraries are developed by the organization's staff to offer participants access to special areas of natural history interest, often inaccessible to the independent traveler. They are designed to help people experience the joy of discovery, meet new friends, and learn about the natural world.

For example, one nature watch research expedition offers the unmatched experience of swimming with pods of free-ranging dolphins while participating in an ongoing research project. Participants study dolphin family and social structure, their behavior and habitat requirements, and modes of communication in the warm waters of the Bahamas, which are ideal for swimmers. There is no other place where wild dolphins can be observed underwater with such consistency and excellent visibility. Since 1984, Oceanic Society Expeditions has been sponsoring dolphin research in this area off Grand Bahama Island among an identifiable group of spotted dolphins. The information gathered promotes a greater understanding of dolphins and is very useful in assisting conservation efforts.

Using only basic snorkel equipment, the group dives and glides among the dolphins, who seem to enjoy human companionship. Trip members must have swimming and snorkeling skills, and some agility is needed, but no special skills or experience are required to participate. Each trip is led by an experienced Oceanic Society naturalist.

There are a variety of other similar nature watch research expeditions that offer ways to experience wild dolphins up close and personally, not as tourists but rather as part of a research team working to unlock the mysteries of these remarkable animals.

Other programs involving only observation include whale watching, tropical birding, spotting polar bears, sea-kayaking, wilderness and overland camping, observing penguins or gorillas, snorkeling, and wildlife safaris. Locations include areas throughout the Americas (e.g., the Caribbean, Baja, California, and Mexico), Africa, Oceania, and Seychelles.

For a free catalog and detailed information call or write to:

Oceanic Society Expeditions
Fort Mason Center, Building E
San Francisco, CA 94123
(800) 326-7491
(415) 441-1106

OUTDOOR VACATIONS FOR WOMEN OVER FORTY

Participants in this program form a diverse group. They are described by a recent vacationer as "tall, short, tiny, heavy, single, married, retired, separated, widowed, divorced, mothers, teachers, lawyers, grandmothers, homemakers, between jobs, very silly, very smart, friendly, quiet, outgoing, and they laugh a lot."

All trips involve physical activity. For some, preconditioning is advised, but women of very different abilities are all accommodated. Everyone has strengths in the outdoors—people just need a chance to discover them.

Most women take the trips by themselves. They come from Maine, Florida, Hawaii, California, Alaska, and all points in between. Participants have varying abilities, skills, and personal challenges; most have little or no experience in the activities to be performed, but experience is not required. What participants do have in common is their desire to be outdoors with others and to have a good time.

Outdoor Vacations for Women Over Forty was founded by Marion Stoddart, an experienced outdoorswoman, trip organizer, and internationally recognized conservationist. In 1987 she received the United Nations Environment Programme's Global Award.

Food and lodging reflect the local color of the trips. Accommodations range from a classic country inn or rustic lodge to a bunk on a sailboat or a sleeping bag under the stars. Food varies from gourmet to country fare. The guides are women who have gained their experience as rangers, naturalists, and instructors for a variety of outdoor organizations.

More than a thousand women from over forty states have vacationed with this organization, and 30 percent have traveled more than once. Some have become inveterate Outdoor Vacations travelers. Most groups are kept small, numbering from ten to sixteen women, and are booked months in advance.

For a brochure and information, write to or call:

Outdoor Vacations for Women Over Forty
P.O. Box 200
Gorton, MA 10450
(508) 448-3331

OUTWARD BOUND

The oldest and largest adventure-based nonprofit educational organization in the world, Outward Bound offers a variety of challenging outdoor programs for fun and achievement. Highly regarded and well known, it began in 1943 providing wilderness and survival trips for children and young adults to build self-discipline, assuredness, self-esteem, and a sense of teamwork. It has since expanded to include special adventures for adults as part of the regular coed courses, along with programs specifically designed for women, couples, and adults age fifty and over.

The adult program allows people to share a wilderness adventure with peers who perhaps are dealing with similar life issues or experiencing parallel life transitions such as retirement. Programs are physically and emotionally challenging, and participants are expected to push themselves to help discover how they can go beyond self-imposed mental and physical limits. No one is required to be a professional outdoorsperson or an athlete. In fact, most who enroll have never set up camp, paddled a canoe or carried a backpack.

The programs lead participants through a sequence of carefully orchestrated, safe activities, teaching skills from a beginner's level. During the adventure, people learn to live comfortably and safely in the wilderness, and to appreciate and protect the outdoors in a way that emphasizes environmental awareness.

Outward Bound's objective is to strive for excellence in everything one does and to discover new confidence in one's ability to face whatever challenges lie ahead. Courses are designed to enhance valuable personal skills in leadership, problem solving, decision making, and communication. The program helps expand a person's sense of self, both as an individual and as a member of a working group.

The courses for adults ages fifty and older are designed for people rich in wisdom and life experience. They emphasize that personal potential, rather than age, should be the measure of their ability to participate. Many in their sixties and seventies have had rewarding and exciting experiences at Outward Bound. Neither age nor limited physical ability have hindered their successful completion of the programs.

Four- to nine-day programs for older adults include canoe expeditioning in the Florida Everglades, canoeing and whitewater rafting on the Rio Grande River in Texas, mountain backpacking and canoeing in the Blue Ridge Mountains of North Carolina, and whitewater rafting on Utah's Green River. Older adults may participate in a variety of interesting courses, not just those tailored for the over-fifty crowd.

For a catalog and further details call or write to:

Outward Bound USA
Route 9D
R2, Box 280
Garrison, NY 10524
(800) 243-8520

OVER THE HILL GANG, INTERNATIONAL

"Once You're Over the Hill, You Pick Up Speed!"

If you're over fifty years young, you're lucky because you can join the gang. The Over the Hill Gang is an international organization, thousands of members strong, created for energetic people who enjoy the camaraderie of year-round activities with their contemporaries and who thrive on an adventurous, active way of life, participating in recreational and social activities.

The Over the Hill Gang started as a ski club years ago but its members now participate in a wide variety of energetic pursuits, such as whitewater rafting, sightseeing adventures, biking, hot air ballooning, soaring, sailing, tennis, golf, skiing, and windjammer cruises. Each event provides opportunities for socializing, touring, relaxing, shopping, and recreational experiences related to the area the members are visiting.

By joining the Over the Hill Gang, International, you are eligible to join one of the many local chapters. You will never lack for company and interesting places to go and things to do as local gangs develop their own activities. Above all, no matter what the activity, the gang offers the opportunity for new friendships and sharing experiences with people your own age. It is not an exclusive singles group either, and doesn't exclude those with spouses under fifty.

Because the club exerts group leverage, resorts and areas will often offer luxurious accommodations at reasonable prices, ski lift and entertainment tickets at reduced rates, and other amenities and discounts.

The annual national membership fee is $37 per person and local membership is assessed based on chapter needs. There is a discount for combined spouse membership as well as for three-year and lifetime memberships.

For further information and an application, call or write to:

Over the Hill Gang, International
3310 Cedar Heights Drive
Colorado Springs, CO 80904
(719) 685-4656

PEACE CORPS

In seventy countries around the globe, over six thousand Americans are serving as Peace Corps volunteers. "Adventurous" certainly describes the increasing number of seniors hard at work at what the agency calls "the toughest job you'll ever love." People over fifty-five now make up about 10 percent of volunteers, a percentage the Peace Corps would like to increase.

Since there is no upper age limit for acceptance into the Peace Corps, from its beginning in 1961 thousands of senior volunteers have brought their skills, talents, and experience to developing countries. Because the elderly are revered in most developing countries, older volunteers immediately command a respect it might take a younger person a year or more to earn.

As satisfying as it is to share your expertise with others, the Peace Corps is not for everyone. The training is rigorous, the hours long, and the job demanding and riddled with frustration. The main reward is that you do make a difference. You also get a chance to travel, an unforgettable living experience in a foreign land; basic expenses and housing; and technical, language, and cultural training. Married couples are certainly eligible and are always assigned together.

Since health, safety, and money are quite naturally of concern to older Americans, the Peace Corps makes ample provisions by providing full medical and dental coverage, a living stipend to meet expenses, a readjustment allowance of $200 for each month on the assigment upon return to the United States, and paid transportation.

Because the process takes time, you should apply at least nine months prior to your availability. If interested call or write to:

The Peace Corps
1990 K Street NW
Washington, DC 20526
(800) 424-8580

You will be sent an application form along with a return envelope,
and a detailed booklet.

RAINBOW ADVENTURES

Worldwide Adventure Travel for Women over Thirty
"Take a Break and Escape"

Not all women of a certain age want to spend their vacations lying
on the beach or sightseeing through the windows of an air-conditioned
car. Some like more challenge: riding a packhorse through Yellowstone
or the Grand Canyon, trekking through the Blue Ridge Mountains
(with a llama to carry gear), whitewater rafting on the Colorado River,
or riding a horse in Ireland or a camel in Kenya.

For over a decade, Rainbow Adventures has been opening the
doors of the world. They have organized outings women would be
unlikely to arrange on their own, and have done it so that these women
don't have to be seasoned, experienced travelers. Their philosophy is
that these adventures should appeal to the novice who has a yen to
see the four corners of the world within an environment that's safe
and comfortable and includes the company of other women with similar
interests.

Seventy percent of Rainbow Adventures' customers have enjoyed
their vacations so much that they've signed up more than once, a
testimony to the quality of service and safety featured on every excursion.
Each of the trips is designed to be active yet relaxing in a way that
allows each woman to enjoy solitude and still mingle and meet with
new friends from around the world.

After years of raising a family or working at a career, women
go to Rainbow Adventures for vacation excitement within an environment that is supportive of their needs. That is why trips are rated from
"easy" to "challenging" so each person can choose her own activity
level and fun. Most of the trips are geared for beginners who want,
but never had the opportunity, to engage in true world exploration.

Clients ranging in age from thirty to seventy, are at a time in their lives when their children are raised; they perhaps are retired or widowed and now want to take a different kind of vacation. Susan Eckert, the owner of Rainbow Adventures, finds that older women are better travelers than younger ones. "They are good-natured realists . . . more flexible and agreeable to accept situations as they exist, which is an extremely important tenet of 'adventure travel.' " Says Ms. Eckert in her brochure, "Rainbow Adventures is for women who want to experience an active vacation, who want to meet new people, and who want to experience a vacation different than the ordinary. Come escape with us!"

To find out more and receive material, call or write to:

Susan Eckert
Rainbow Adventures
1308 Sherman Avenue
Evanston, IL 60201
(800) 804-8686
(708) 864-4570

SAGA INTERNATIONAL HOLIDAYS

Quality Worldwide Travel

Saga Holidays, a direct-mail travel company founded in England, has provided travel opportunities for mature, quality-minded travelers since the 1950s. It is the largest company in its field, specializing in meeting the travel needs of people sixty and over (an accompanying spouse or friend may be fifty or over). In 1985 and 1989 Saga Holidays received the Queen's Award for Export Achievement—one of the very few companies in the travel industry to have earned this prestigious award.

Saga Holidays has provided quality worldwide travel to hundreds of thousands of people from its offices in Boston, Massachusetts; Folkestone, England; and Sydney, Australia. All trips are arranged directly with the company and its holiday specialists, as opposed to travel agents. On some holidays Americans may encounter fellow travelers from Great Britain and Australia: this interesting blend from a variety of cultures is an attractive extra benefit for many Saga customers.

The biggest contributor to Saga's consistent success is the level of quality and value it provides in its holidays and services. Says a representative of the company: "People associate Saga Holidays with quality and we do everything we can to keep it this way. We make sure everything about the tour—from accommodations and meals to transportation and the tour director—meets our standards. If it doesn't, it isn't part of the tour. Our vast experience in planning tours gives us the edge we need to put together a higher quality travel experience for a lower cost."

Saga Holidays operates tours in Australia, New Zealand, and the South Pacific; Asia and Africa; Great Britain and Ireland; Europe and the former Soviet Union; the United States and Canada; and Mexico and Central and South America. A wide variety of cruise holidays are also available to destinations throughout the world. Saga Holidays likewise operates educational "Smithsonian Odyssey Tours" in a joint arrangement with the Smithsonian Institution, as well as tours of "Gardens of the World" in conjunction with the White Flower Farm of Litchfield, Connecticut. Both types of specialty tours offer exciting holiday opportunities as well as unique learning experiences.

Special features of a Saga holiday include: guaranteed inclusive prices, departures from many cities throughout the United States, medical and flight insurance, tour escorts and/or local guides, refunds for cancellations due to medical reasons, and the offer to match single travelers with a roommate.

For further information and free brochures, call or write to:

Saga International Holidays, Ltd.
222 Berkeley Street
Boston, MA 02116
(800) 343-0273
Mondays—Fridays: 9 A.M.–7 P.M.
Saturdays: 10 A.M.–4 P.M.

SCORE

The Service Corps of Retired Executives Association

SCORE, administered by the United States Small Business Administration, provides counseling to small business owners and community organizations. It is made up of over 13,000 retired and working executives who volunteer their time and business expertise to help today's generation of fledgling entrepreneurs. SCORE counselors provide one-on-one team counseling to people who wish to start a business or are already in an enterprise and need assistance. Counselors also develop and conduct business seminars on a wide range of topics.

Since many people in retirement miss the challenges of their previous business life, this is an opportunity for them to use their skills to help someone establish a business, solve operational problems, or perhaps expand a growing business. Skills and experience in business planning, marketing, retailing and merchandising, engineering, business startup or expansion, financing, manufacturing, or other aspects of small business management are also valuable in becoming a SCORE volunteer. Most of the time volunteers work at the chapter closest to their residences.

For an application, additional information, and the location of the chapter nearest you, call or write to:

SCORE
409 3rd Street SW
Washington, D.C. 20024-3212
(800) 634-0245

SHELTER INSTITUTE

Learning Housebuilding

Want to learn how to build or repair a house for a quarter to half of the national average cost? Head for the Shelter Institute in Bath, Maine, as many people have.

Since 1974, more than 20,000 people of all ages, shapes, and sizes have come from every state and most foreign countries for many reasons. They will distinguish themselves and the houses they build or fix up by their own verve. They come alone, in twos and threes, or as a group: a couple in foreign service on home leave wanted to build when they retire in five years; a Virginia couple in their seventies wanted a summer home in Maine; a divorced New York City librarian wanted to build on a beautiful piece of land in Vermont; a divorced Wisconsin superintendent of schools wanted a retirement home on the upper peninsula of Michigan; a postman wanted a house easy to heat yet large enough to accommodate his visiting grandchildren; a Dupont executive wanted to build on a family island in Maine; a retiring school teacher and her robust son wanted to build a home in Montana. Participants range in age from college students to individuals in their eighties.

If you have $675 for tuition and three weeks to spare, you can learn everything from site selection and design considerations to engineering and the physics of materials, plumbing, electricity, and framing. If you're in a hurry, take the two-week, condensed course for $625. For those who simply wish to learn timber framing, a one-week program to cut and erect a whole post and beam frame costs $400.

Why travel all the way to Maine when adult-education programs and the Board of Cooperative Educational Services (BOCES) offer construction and house-building courses? Because the Shelter Institute does it better, most distinctively by having its students actually pound the nails and caulk the cracks at a variety of nearby housing sites. The emphasis is on energy efficiency and cost savings, with students learning ingenious ways to save money on materials and techniques. The owners say there is no program like this in the country. It includes all the systems of the house, including all the different framing patterns, from 16" on center to post and beam. Two-thirds of the institute's 20,000 graduates have built new houses and one third have renovated or repaired existing structures. The goal is to understand the house in order to save money in construction and long-term maintenance.

More is taught than there is actually time for. Students choose daily between workshops and house site work to accommodate their learning needs: new house construction, old house restoration, or energy update. Shelter Institute has designed its courses to demystify the house.

In 1991 the Shelter Institute opened its new sixty-eight-acre campus. It is a beautiful, wooded site with unlimited hands-on opportunities.

For detailed information and brochures, call or write to:

> Shelter Institute
> 38 Center Street
> Bath, ME 04530
> (207) 442-7938

SOLO FLIGHTS AND MATURE TOURS

Catering to Single Vacationers

This travel center, founded in 1974, specializes in vacations for the single traveler of all ages, with a significant proportion of its clientele being over fifty.

For many people, the idea of solo travel is a little frightening. It's unnerving to contemplate moving through airports, customs, currency exchanges, strange hotel rooms, and dining rooms completely on one's own. Finding a friend to go where and when the traveler wishes can be a discouraging process. Too often friends back out after the plans are made.

Solo Flights says that the safest way for a lone traveler to go is with a group of older singles, or even a mixed group. For those wanting to save on high-cost single room accommodations, room-sharing arrangements can usually be made. Those concerned about sharing a room with a "stranger" should consider the fact that these arrangements work out very well since a total stranger can be a better travel mate than a long-time friend. To begin with, you don't have to think of your relationship after the trip, unless a friendship does develop. Being candid often comes more easily with a stranger; there tends to be less dependency on and feeling of responsibility to the other person. For those who are not actually loners but who absolutely want to be alone at bedtime, the extra cost of a single room is well spent.

Travel groups are often divided into "under 35" and "over 35" or "mixed ages," the latter two including many senior citizens. Solo Flights has found that the age differences are unimportant on a trip; the trip itself becomes the common denominator. Although one need not restrict oneself to single companions, it is more comfortable for the single traveler to share experiences with others going it alone than to be surrounded by couples.

There is absolutely no charge for Solo Flights personal consultation service. Those at Solo Flights makes it their business to be aware of the best tours, cruises, packages, groups, and rates for single people.

Call from 10 A.M. to 10 P.M., Monday through Friday, and until noon on Saturday; you'll speak to a travel consultant who will help you find the vacation that best suits your individual travel needs, from weekend getaways to full-scale vacations. Solo Flights will handle every step, from contacting the tour operator and reserving space on the cruise line to making your airline reservations. Ask for Betty Sobol, founder and director of Solo Flights, who has vast experience in the travel field for singles. Call or write to:

Solo Flights
127 South Compo Road
Westport, CT 06880
(203) 226-9993

TRAVLTIPS

Cruise & Freighter Travel Association
"Roam the World by Freighter"

For the traveler with a sense of adventure, freighter travel is the perfect way to visit famous ports of call as well as places off the beaten track untouched by modern commercialism. The best of both worlds awaits the freighter traveler.

Traveling by freighter is a fascinating, first-class way to roam the world, often for half the cost per day of a regular cruise. Freighters are for travelers, not tourists, who want unregimented days at sea without the endless "game show" activities now common aboard conventional ocean liners. The atmosphere aboard a freighter is unstructured and relaxing.

Once aboard, you'll find your dozen or so companions to be well-rounded, perceptive people who know what they want when they travel. There's time to read, to feel the majesty of the sea, to observe the activities of a working cargo ship, and to relax with interesting people—retired professionals, writers, teachers, or the self-employed—all free from the constraints of a scheduled vacation.

Since freighters are primarily working ships, itineraries are regulated by cargo schedules. Sailing dates may be revised several times and ports of call changed, so voyage lengths are usually given as an average range of days. Retired freighter enthusiasts who are flexible in their travel time relish this spontaneity and the excitement that comes with an unpredictable schedule. To them, this means adventure and the romance of travel.

Most people don't know that accommodations aboard a freighter are equal to, or often superior to, higher-priced staterooms found on deluxe passenger liners. Most are spacious outside cabins high above the sea, with large windows rather than portholes, and private bathrooms, some with tubs. Typically, you'll sail with about twelve passengers and share a dining room and comfortable lounge with the ship's officers. Other public areas on most freighters include a comfortable lounge with VCR and stereo; a library and recreation room; and an outside deck with lounge chairs for sunning, reading, or getting acquainted with fellow passengers. Some cargo ships even have small swimming pools.

Good, plentiful meals are served three times a day, with menus ranging from the national cuisine of the line to familiar American fare. Fresh baked goods are common, and most freighters have a pantry for between-meal snacks.

TravLtips Cruise & Freighter Travel is a membership organization offering low-cost, value-oriented travel aboard a cargo-carrying freighter or cruise ship to unique and unusual destinations. Many cruise programs are on expedition-type vessels that can access seldom-visited areas to give small numbers of passengers insights into the culture and natural history of the destination. Retirees are usually very interested in educational trips and these have become increasingly popular.

Since these travel opportunities are not advertised in the newspaper and typically not available through regular agents or tour promoters, for more information you should call or write to:

> TravLtips
> Cruise & Freighter Travel Association
> P.O. Box 218
> Flushing, NY 11358
> (718) 939-2400

Membership is $30 per year, which includes a variety of benefits and a subscription to the association's magazine.

UNIVERSITY RESEARCH EXPEDITIONS

Contribute to Understanding Life on This Planet

The University Research Expeditions Program (UREP) invites people to share the challenges and rewards of scientific discovery as a member of University of California research expeditions. No special academic or field experience is necessary to participate; curiosity, adaptability, and a willingness to share the costs and lend a helping hand are the most important qualifications. Expedition teams investigate everything from ways to ensure that tropical forests are preserved for the next generation to uncovering clues to the past through excavations of archaeological sites dating from medieval times to over ten thousand years ago.

UREP's mission is to build a partnership for achieving an understanding the past and how it can help ensure a better and sustainable future for all inhabitants of this planet. Each participant on an expedition becomes an active member of the field team and contributes an equal share to cover project costs. As a donation to the University of California, this contribution of about $1,400, which covers all expenses, except airfare, for a two-week expedition, is tax-deductible. In return for their assistance and support, participants have an opportunity to gain new skills, new friends, and insights into other cultures while experiencing firsthand the excitement of scientific discovery.

The expeditions offer a variety of interesting field research in archaeology, natural resources conservation, environmental studies, arts and culture, and earth sciences in Europe, Africa, Central and South America, and the United States. Participants, including many retirees, come from all areas of the United States. People considering the program are invited to call past participants to hear firsthand what a UREP adventure is like.

For a brochure and other detailed information write or call:

University Research Expeditions Program
University of California
Berkeley, CA 94720
(510) 642-6586

VACATION EXCHANGE CLUB

Rent-Free Vacations Worldwide

The Vacation Exchange Club, established in 1960, is a worldwide membership of individuals and families who enjoy the unique benefits of exchanging homes for holidays each year. The organization has about

16,000 members in fifty countries, predominantly in North America and Europe. Most members are professionals, business executives, and retirees.

Four times a year the Club publishes a directory describing available homes, with photographs and holiday preferences of members seeking a home-swap holiday during the current year. On receipt of the directory, you simply select a few listings that meet your requirements and then contact the listed members. Once you decide to swap homes with another member you both then write to each other to confirm the details. The directories include simple step-by-step guidance on what to do during each stage of an exchange; members can call Vacation Exchange Club at any time for more information or advice.

As guests in each other's homes, both partners in an exchange enjoy that special bond of mutual respect and trust that the situation generates. The Vacation Exchange Club reports that in over thirty years of exchanging, there have been very few instances of damage and no reports of theft. Houses are invariably left just as they were found. Members are in direct contact with each other through letters and by phone while arranging the holiday, and will be on friendly, first-name terms by the time the exchange takes place. Home insurance companies are usually delighted to hear that you have arranged for guests to stay in your home while you are away on holiday. They prefer that a house be occupied rather than left empty.

Members receive a unique reference number for the current year that identifies them to others as a member; this ensures that only bona fide members are using the directories. It is through this system that the club is able to monitor and safeguard its high reputation for home exchanging and maintain the trust and respect that has developed between Vacation Exchange Club members.

There are no arrangement fees, no extra costs, no hidden charges, just a membership fee that includes the books of holiday exchange offers from members all over the world. Some members swap homes many times a year and offer country club privileges, the family motorhome, sports club facilities, and other comforts. Club literature describes one couple from Rye, New York, on their way to Surrey, England, having exchanged their home for a small castle in Scotland the year before. Another couple recalled their previous summer vacation in a luxury apartment in Belgium and was looking forward to another exchange, this time in a Telluride, Colorado, home. One San Francisco family arrived in their Winnipeg, Ontario, exchange home to find a bottle of champagne waiting for them and fresh flowers throughout the house.

For an information packet call or write to:

Vacation Exchange Club
P.O. Box 650
Key West, FL 33041
(800) 638-3841

VINTAGE AIR TOURS

Flights of Nostalgia

Experience a place in time when travel was still an adventure. Climb aboard an elegant, fully restored, air-conditioned, twin-engine DC-3 airplane and suddenly you are back in 1945 bound for a tropical island. The atmosphere is pure nostalgia with classic 1940s-issue flight crew's uniforms, memorable music from the past, and even vintage *Life* and *Look* magazines. Once on board, passengers are treated to champagne service and spectacular aerial views through large picture windows that provide unique photographic opportunities.

Vintage Air Tours is certified by the Federal Aviation Administration and offers all-inclusive day and overnight packages to Key West, recreating the nostalgia of the 1940s with first-class service and comfortable seating. While en route, passengers are welcome to visit the cockpit and sit in the jump seat for a personal chat with the pilots.

For $27 per person the Key West Adventure package includes: a first-class preflight continental breakfast; round trip airfares; in-flight champagne; trolley transfers to and from the airport; lunch in old town Key West, and a choice of two great island activities. Vintage Air Tours also arranges a variety of overnight options and other activities, and operates four days per week (Wednesday, Friday, Saturday, and Sunday). The flight departs Kissimmee Municipal Airport in the morning and the return flight departs about one hour after sunset.

For information, call or write to:

Vintage Air Tours
310 N. Dyer Boulevard
Suite 316
Kissimmee, FL 34741
(800) U-FLY-DC-3

VOLUNTEERS IN SERVICE TO AMERICA (VISTA)

Helping People Help Themselves

VISTA is a full-time, year-long volunteer program for men and women from all backgrounds committed to increasing the ability of low-income people to improve the conditions of their own lives. Volunteers are assigned to local sponsors, which may be state or local public agencies or private nonprofit organizations located in the fifty states.

Volunteers live among the poor, serving in urban and rural areas. They share their skills and experience in fields such as drug abuse, literacy, health, employment training, food distribution, shelter for the homeless, and neighborhood revitalization. Volunteers may serve in their home community or in other parts of the country. The volunteer's role in the poverty problem-solving process is focused on mobilizing community resources and increasing the capacity of the target community to solve its own problems. While VISTA serves as an important link between the local sponsor and the people being served, it adheres to the concept of local self-reliance. Sponsoring organizations plan for the eventual phase-out of VISTA volunteers and for the performance of the VISTA volunteers' function by local citizens.

VISTA is part of AmeriCorps, the U.S. government umbrella organization for domestic volunteer service. VISTA pays travel expenses and provides some relocation assistance for volunteers who serve outside their local community. All volunteers receive preservice training, typically a four-day session providing an orientation to the VISTA program, terms and benefits of VISTA service, and the generic skills needed to perform the assignment. During the assignment, volunteers receive additional training.

While people don't become VISTA volunteers to get rich, there are financial benefits such as a monthly living allowance to cover the cost of food, housing, and incidentals. A stipend is also paid for each month of service at the completion of the assignment.

Serving with VISTA can be a challenging opportunity for retirees and others to share their skills. Intangible benefits include the sense of personal growth and satisfaction that comes from helping bring about significant changes in other people's lives.

For an information packet and an application, call or write to:

Americorps/VISTA
1100 Vermont Avenue NW
Washington, D.C. 20525
(800) 424-8867

WINDJAMMING

A Unique Sea Adventure

To those who want to go down to the sea again (or for the first time); who find romance in the whipcrack of a taut sail, the swish of a ship's bow cutting through the water; and who are drawn to an unbuckled life on the bounding main . . . welcome to the world of windjammers.

Picture this: A hundred-foot wooden ship with sails filled, plowing through the chill, clear waters off the coast of Maine toward a secluded cove on a spruce-covered island.

Taste this: A bowl of fish chowder, a pot roast with three vegetables, home-baked oatmeal bread, a salad, two kinds of pie and a fruit bowl—just one of three such meals a day.

Imagine this: All hands on deck to lower the sails as the second mate sings a chantey, then crewing a dinghy to row ashore for a lobster and clambake under sunny skies on an uninhabited island.

This is a different world, a windship's world. No engines, phones, televisions, or mail calls, only sails and wind, and islands that cut the rim of the sea.

A windjammer is a turn-of-the-century term for the coastal passenger and cargo ships that ultimately lost out to steamboats. Some have been found and restored. The *Heritage,* bigger than most other schooners, was built just nine years ago from old plans modified to provide greater creature comforts; ninety-four feet long and twenty-four feet wide, it provides lots of space for everyone. The schooner is very stable, so sea sickness is seldom a liability even when sailing hard. Being large with high rails the *Heritage* feels safe, comfortable, and roomy. Also, being a "coasting schooner," the ship purposely is not very deep in the water, which allows it to anchor in those tiny, picturesque coves and harbors people have heard so much about. The *Heritage* and the twelve other windjammers that comprise the Maine Windjammer Association sail from a number of Maine ports from June through September, leaving Monday mornings and returning Saturday.

All cruises are for one week: time enough to get to know the other shipmates and just time enough to sample all the different galley delights. The schooner is always anchoring to explore islands and see birds and wildlife. A passenger can help hoist and furl the sails, coil the lines, cat the anchor, or take the helm; or, if he or she prefers, just stretch out on the deck and enjoy the sun or curl up with a good book.

An ambience of friendly relaxation rules the day. The crew of eight and thirty-three passengers, many being retirees, share a delightful week-long voyage under sail along the coast of Maine. Spruce-capped islands, seal-covered ledges, peaceful saltwater coves, and some of the best traditionally home-cooked meals a person has ever eaten contribute to a unique experience.

For color brochures and detailed information, call or write to:

Windjamming
Box 482
Rockland, ME 04841
(207) 594-8007
(800) 648-4544

WOMANSHIP

Sailing Programs Designed by Women for Women

Womanship is a year-round, accredited organization recognized through-out the sailing world. Based in Annapolis, Maryland, it employs only female instructors. They have collectively taught more than five thousand people how to sail since opening in 1985. Womanship is a practical experience in a learning environment where (says their motto) "nobody yells."

Courses are designed for people at all levels, from beginner sailors to those with considerable experience. Students range in age from eighteen to seventy-five. They are doctors, waitresses, account executives, those in the service, pregnant women, and, of course, many retired people.

With Womanship, the boat is the classroom. Learning is gentle, reassuring, and nontraumatically achieved by "doing" under natural conditions—just the way sailors have learned through the ages. Expertly guided by patient instructors, students apply what they learn at their own pace in a sequence of hands-on learning experiences that lead to real understanding and self-reliance.

Womanship instructors are chosen not only for their sailing skills, patience, and maturity but for their demonstrated ability to enable each student to experience the thrill of accomplishment that comes with learning for herself and succeeding in taking charge. Their pleasure in teaching comes from sharing their knowledge and in finding the teaching moment that brings the light into each student's eyes. Womanship instructors hold credentials from U.S. and Canadian yachting associations and have U.S. Coast Guard captain's licenses.

As one female student said: "Womanship was more than my introduction to sailing. It heightened my appreciation of life on the water. There's something different about viewing a sunset from there, watching the water turn a deep gold and the sky fade to midnight. I felt a part of it." And another, "Thank God for Womanship. I have been sailing for years with my husband and never felt confident until now."

Womanship teaching centers are located in Annapolis/Chesapeake Bay, Florida, New England, Long Island Sound, the Pacific Northwest, and the Virgin Islands.

Sailboats used are suited to the waters where the learning cruises sail. Well-built performance cruisers are chosen to be responsive for teaching, yet provide comfortable accommodations and living space.

Two- and three-day daytime cruise courses are available, as are live-aboard cruises from two to ten days and specially customized courses for couples, families and groups, younger women (ages eleven to seventeen), and mothers and teenaged daughters.

For information and materials, call or write to:

Womanship
The Boat House
410 Severn Avenue
Annapolis, MD 21403
(410) 267-6661
(800) 342-9295

Many of the organizations and activities in this chapter I or family and friends have personally reviewed. Each one is unique and can offer you the opportunity to try something new, as well as the freedom to grow in a direction you choose. I hope you experience some of them.

Retirement has its peaks and valleys, ups and downs, just like the rest of life. This exciting chapter of life can be filled with exploring new pursuits, learning different skills, making new friends, and having the time to enjoy it all.

Remember how we used to measure our age? "I just hit the big thirty." "It's difficult to believe that I am actually forty years old!"; "I'm at the half century milestone, but it doesn't feel so bad"; "I'm almost sixty and I don't feel much different than when I was thirty-five. To tell you the truth, I feel better than ever. I'm more active than I have been for years." Our feelings and attitudes about ourselves, our families, our friends, and our lives are the most enduring and positive forces for dealing with what life gives us. Age is merely a number; our spirit can remain young forever.

12

Retirement Planning Checklist: Major Activities and Issues

Retirement should be a meaningful and exciting experience, and it can be! Great retirements don't just happen, they are planned. They require careful deliberation and making choices.

Retirement planning at its best is a gradual and ongoing process that you cannot complete all at one time. At some point during your career years, whether as a homemaker or out in the workforce, you may dream about the freedom and fulfillment retirement will bring. Actually experiencing the personal satisfaction is a different matter— something too important to leave to chance. Without proper planning, retirement can be troubling and worrisome for many people. Retirement, or your "next chapter," is a relatively new social phenomenon in American society, one which many of us are unfamiliar. It's like another career and needs to be carefully approached and managed that way.

Whatever your age today, it isn't too early to begin the tasks included in this chapter. The checklists contained here are outlines of many of the things you need to be aware of. It is a good idea to review these lists and occasionally gauge your progress toward your retirement objectives. By the time you are retired, you will have an active and well thought-out program for each of the areas on the list. You will be beginning to experience the adventure of retirement!

FINANCES AND LEGAL MATTERS

Our research shows that money heads the list of factors required for a successful and productive retirement. Like the other ingredients on this checklist, financial security does require preplanning; yet we know that many people at retirement age are neither confident nor in control of their finances.

A large number of economic and demographic changes are requiring preretirees to need more cash at the end of their careers than they previously thought would be necessary. For example, Social Security taxes and health costs represent a bigger deduction from preretirement salaries than ever before. Soaring college tuition, delayed marriages, late parenting, and a difficult job market for new graduates find more people still supporting their children while, at the same time, striving to save money for their retirement. In addition, since people are living longer and the quality of that longer life is better than ever, enjoying retirement for thirty to forty years isn't unusual. People need money for that length of time.

It's your money and you're the one who must make it last. Part of the strategy is knowing your financial position before retirement and being able to make the necessary choices and adjustments ahead of time. Run through the following checklist:

1. _____ I have determined my current annual expenses in key budget categories.

2. _____ I have calculated my annual retirement budget, in today's dollars, by examining each category and determining what expenses will increase or decrease in retirement.

3. _____ I have adjusted my estimated retirement expenses by using an assumed rate of inflation for the future. In other words, my expenses will continue to increase because inflation will also.

4. _____ I have determined how much of this amount will be provided by my retirement benefits, for example, from company plans and Social Security.

5. _____ I now know how much additional retirement income, if any, I need in order to meet my expenses in retirement.

6. _____ If my retirement expenses exceed my retirement income, I know what options are available to me to balance the shortfall.

7. _____ I have calculated my present net worth and how much my assets will be worth at the time I retire.

8. _____ I have decided the most appropriate way to take the distributions from my company savings plan and any other qualified plans.

9. _____ I know what my retirement tax bracket will be because my spendable income is determined by it.

10. _____ I have made arrangements to educate myself about taxes, investing, and other aspects of personal finance by enrolling in adult education classes at local colleges or high schools, reviewing some of the many financial newsletters available, and noting other programs available, for example, through my bank or the local YMCA.

11. _____ I have reviewed my investment options, such as IRAs, stocks and bonds, CDs, mutual funds, and money market accounts, to ensure a balanced portfolio.

12. _____ Before I invest in something, I will know and understand the following:
   • What does it cost?
   • How much does it pay; what is its yield?
   • What are the risks?
   • Can I access my money if I need it before retirement?
   • How long do I need to leave it in before maturity?
   • How is it taxed?

13. _____ I have completed a valid, current will and discussed it with my attorney.

14. _____ I have taken time to understand and, if necessary, arrange, for a living will,* a health proxy form,† and durable power of attorney.‡

15. _____ I have evaluated my life insurance coverage in a way that responds to my present and future family needs.

16. _____ I have made provisions for my medical insurance coverage in retirement and know how it integrates with Medicare.

DISCRETIONARY TIME

How retirees spend their time is one of the most important ingredients in a satisfying retirement. Research reveals that many retirees accomplish in a very short time all the things they had been planning for the last thirty-five years. Many get very good at doing just nothing. So, imagine your life as a retiree: Think what an average day or week would be like after the initial six months to one year of "catching up on things" or "smelling the roses."

Retirement brings with it a great deal of freedom, offering about fifty hours a week of increased time. Therefore, people should develop activities that satisfy their needs for growth, relaxation, recreation, self-

---

*A *living will* expresses your feelings to those you love and to the legal authorities concerning the continuation of your life and possible participation in the organ donation program in the event you are mentally or physically incapacitated. This form requires two witnesses and must be notarized.

†A *health proxy form* enables you to protect your health care wishes by assigning an agent, someone you love and trust, to decide about medical treatment on your behalf when you are unable to decide for yourself. This form requires two witnesses and can be completed without the assistance of an attorney.

‡A *durable power of attorney* conveys authority to a trusted family member or friend to direct and manage your financial affairs for you in the event you are unable to do so. Because a durable power of attorney conveys broad powers to another party, this form is best completed with the assistance of an attorney; however, it can be completed using a notary public. This power goes into effect under conditions you have previously decided and remains in effect during your incapacity. A durable power of attorney is often preferred over a regular power of attorney, whose authority ceases when you become disabled, requiring a court-appointed conservator to look after your affairs. Conservatorship rights can be costly and time-consuming, and the court may not appoint the person you would prefer to have manage your affairs.

expression, participation, recognition, adventure, learning, health, security, and whatever else is important to their well-being.

1. _____ I understand that it is possible to have a total of 40,000 to 80,000 hours' free time when I retire.

2. _____ I have begun seriously thinking about what goals and objectives I would like to achieve in retirement.

3. _____ I have some reasonably clear ideas about how I plan to spend my discretionary retirement time.

4. _____ I have considered which of my current activities I would like to continue after my work life is completed.

5. _____ I have explored alternative pursuits, done research, and arranged for classes or other training that will help me obtain more enjoyment out of life.

6. _____ I have connected with people whose skills and talents I admire by joining professional organizations.

7. _____ I have considered the possibility of a second career in a new field that interests me, on either a part-time or full-time basis.

8. _____ I have investigated the numerous satisfying opportunities for volunteering, or for starting my own business. I have begun the process of fulfilling my ambitions in these areas.

9. _____ I have already found a useful postretirement role.

RELOCATION AND HOUSING

Believe it or not, most retirees stay put; about 85 to 90 percent keep the family home or stay within a ten-mile radius. People's roots are too deep to be casually pulled up; when they live in one place for so long, their home becomes part of them and is so filled with memories that it becomes more than a mere asset to be traded away. Most people want to remain near friends and neighbors, to stay in their churches, clubs, and organizations, and to continue doing business in the banks and stores they are accustomed to. Those who do move may relocate more than once or even return to their original locations.

If you do move, the new home should be an improvement and/ or have an advantage over your present location. Your alternatives are endless, and choosing a new location to settle in can be exciting, but you might want to take a few years to investigate before you decide. If you think through your choices carefully, act on them slowly and reflectively, you will have a better chance of being satisfied with the outcome. Include the following considerations:

1. _____ I have considered my present community to ascertain how suitable it would be as a retirement location.

2. _____ I have considered moving to:
   - Live in a nicer area
   - Live in a safer neighborhood
   - Have a house of a more appropriate size
   - Reduce the cost and responsibilities of maintaining a home
   - Reduce property taxes
   - Take a new job
   - Build a new home
   - Be in a more healthful environment
   - Be closer to family members and friends
   - Be in a better climate
   - Be nearer to cultural and recreational facilities
   - Enjoy a change of scenery
   - Be closer to quality medical services
   - Have access to special services for older people.

3. _____ I have decided on some possible retirement locations.

4. _____ I have investigated these locations in detail, visited them at different times of the year, and am very familiar with them.

5. _____ I have talked with other retirees in these potential new areas and asked them what they like and dislike.

6. _____ I am confident that the new location I have selected offers services that will meet my needs.

7. _____ I have researched the variety of housing alternatives available not only for my current needs but also for the future, including:
- Condominiums
- Retirement communities
- Mobile homes
- Apartments
- Residence exchange clubs
- Cooperatives
- Single-family homes
- Accessory apartments: complete, new living units installed in a single-family home, often for older parents
- Home matching and shared housing
- Lifecare communities: long-term living arrangements where housing and total care (meals, housekeeping, transportation, recreation, and health and nursing services) are purchased for a substantial fee in addition to monthly payments. These are particularly suited to elderly and older adults.

FITNESS AND HEALTH

If people don't have their health, they will not have the energy to enjoy a full commitment to their retirement. Although they cannot change their genetic makeup, people can control many aspects of their lives, which may lead to a longer life, free from the common fears of aging.

If you have good health you can do just about anything. Being healthy is rarely a happy accident, though it costs almost nothing, as anyone with good health will confirm. More people today in retirement are experiencing positive health because they are taking control of it and have an optimistic attitude. Because of this, people are living longer today than ever before, passionate and forceful to the end rather than gradually declining into dependency. Check your own health care attitudes and habits against the following checklist:

1. _____ I would like to live as long as possible provided I am healthy.

2. _____ I understand that a positive lifestyle is a significant contribution to a long and healthy life.

3. _____ I have recently had a physical examination.

4. _____ I have made exercise a natural, enjoyable part of my life, and have incorporated into my schedule a regular exercise program emphasizing cardiovascular and strength training. (The National Institutes of Health have shown exercise to be the most effective anti-aging method known.)

5. _____ I have changed my eating habits to minimize health risks and make good nutritional choices. My daily food choices emphasize:
   - Low cholesterol and fat, especially saturated fat, found primarily foods derived from animals
   - Low sodium
   - Moderate protein
   - A good suppy of calcium
   - High complex carbohydrates and fiber, such as those found in whole grains, fresh fruits, and fresh vegetables.

6. _____ I have assessed my personal habits and behaviors and their effect on my health, and made a real effort to improve them where necessary.

7. _____ I am aware of the techniques of preventive medicine, and have established a cooperative health care partnership with my physician, including regular medical screenings.

SPOUSE/PARTNER

When people retire, they don't withdraw into a vacuum but into a nesting of relationships, the primary relationship being with the spouse or person with whom the retiree will spend a major portion of his or her retirement time. Generally relationships change during retirement—significantly for some and slightly for others.

Our research shows that those people who invest time *before* they retire discussing with one another their expectations, plans, and the changes that may occur during retirement, tend to have a more satisfying relationship after retirement with fewer misunderstandings and surprises. Through a process of discussion and self-examination, people at midlife can benefit from recognizing what they can change and how to deal with and compromise about those things that will not change. Help determine your relationship's suitability for retirement by going through the following checklist:

1. _____ I have discussed my plans and expectations for retirement with my spouse or the person with whom I plan to spend some of my retirement.

2. _____ I have talked with my spouse (or significant other) about whether we want to retire at the same time.

3. _____ My spouse (or significant other) and I have discussed our needs as a couple and individually to ascertain our schedules during retirement.

4. _____ If we decide not to retire at the same time, we have discussed what changes may occur in handling household tasks.

5. _____ If we do decide to retire at the same time, I am willing to share the household tasks.

6. _____ I have discussed with my spouse (or significant other) how we will spend my earnings if I continue to work.

7. _____ Will I feel guilty during the working day when my spouse (or significant other) is home alone?

8. _____ Would I object to my spouse's (or significant other's) getting a job when I retire?

9. _____ Would I be willing to accept some domestic duties if my spouse (or significant other) works when I am retired?

10. _____ Do I expect my spouse (or significant other) to do many of the things he or she always did in the daytime and not change his or her routine when I am home?

11. _____ I have discussed with my spouse (or significant other) my expectations about the second half of our life—about our emotional, sexual, and physical needs.

12. _____ Do I assume that my spouse (or significant other) will spend all of his or her daytime and evening hours with me following retirement?

13. _____ I have planned some activities separately from my partner because this promotes togetherness. It reduces the "What's new? Nothing" pitfall.

CAREGIVING CONSIDERATIONS

As America's older population continues to increase, elder care is becoming one of the issues most commonly discussed by government, business, and the media. Ironically, an estimated 83 percent of American families never discuss elder care arrangements in advance.

If you have a parent alive today, you may in the future become involved in some aspect of your aging parent's care. Your parent problem may be financial, medical, or emotional. Often it will be all three at once, and inevitably you will be central to the solution. However you choose to lend your support, whether with money, time, or a compassionate blend of both, the effect upon your life will undoubtedly be significant.

Unanticipated caregiving disrupts the most carefully planned retirements. However, reacting to this type of emergency becomes much easier if options are established in advance.

1. _____ I have thought about who will care for my parents or relatives if they become disabled.

2. _____ I have reviewed who the best candidate in the family is to provide or arrange for care.

3. _____ If my parents or relatives live a distance away, how will I handle their needs?

4. _____ What expectations do I have of my spouse or children concerning caring for my parents or relatives?

5. _____ I have considered what types of assistance I may require if I were to be responsible for the complete care of a parent or relative.

6. _____ I am aware of the variety of community resources that could help me in the role of a caregiver should it become necessary.

7. _____ I have determined whether I would need to change or modify my retirement activities should I assume caregiving responsibilities.

8. _____ I have suggested ways to make my parents' home more comfortable and safer if they are experiencing diminished physical abilities in movement, strength, dexterity, eyesight, or hearing.

13

Educate Yourself:
An Annotated Subject Bibliography

"More attention must be given to the psychological aspects of retirement. Many, and I'm one, spent years in school learning; then we achieved identity, power, recognition, etc. in work, which, upon retirement, vanishes before the retirement letter ink is dry. We fail somehow to perceive how inextricably interwoven our identity is with our profession and we know so little and are ill-prepared for the long stretch of retirement."

"Retirement is a very personal life transformation and it is important to begin self-exploration by learning as much as we can. Self-esteem and knowledge is essential if individuals are going to make meaningful adjustments to severely altered time and social patterns. It has truly been an adventure for us."

I used a variety of sources to compile the following bibliography. First of all I have a large personal library of publications I have accumulated; I read extensively books from the library and keep records along with my own brief review; I have access to numerous publications, reviews, and opinions through membership with professional organizations and the Prometheus Golden Age Books catalogue.

ADJUSTMENT

Bradford, Leland P. and Martha I. *Retirement: Coping with Emotional Upheavals*. Chicago: Nelson-Hall, 1979.
Discusses four problem areas in retirement: unexpected shocks, losses and displacements, the need for a planned transition, and marital adjustments. Suggests strategies for self-acceptance, better communication, and mutual support, based upon the authors' personal experiences.

Bridges, William. *Transitions*. Reading, Mass.: Addison-Wesley, 1980.
A deceptively simple, creative analysis of the process of change experienced by adults coping with the retirement transition process. Suggests soothing strategies for coping with difficult, painful, and confusing times.

Falk, Ursula A., Ph.D. *On Our Own: Independent Living for Older Persons*. Buffalo, N.Y.: Prometheus Books, 1989.
Offers practical information on many aspects of solo living: the emotional stress of loneliness and boredom, handling financial difficulties, developing new relationships, family support systems, employment opportunities, community resources and how to find them, and physical security and safety.

Lieberman, Morton A., and Sheldon S. Tobin. *The Experience of Old Age*. New York: Basic Books, 1983.
The authors, who are social scientists, examine the effects of crisis: relocation, losses, the awareness that life is terminating. They document the central issue of late life: maintaining selfhood, i.e., a sense of self-continuity, self-integrity, and self-identity. They suggest strategies to achieve this.

Nelson, Pearl A. *The First Year: A Retirement Journal*. Buffalo, N.Y.: Potentials Development for Health and Aging Services, 1981.
Relates how one retiree comes to realize that she must find new ways to find happiness. Chronicles an emerging philosophy of finding something to do, something to love, and something to hope for.

AGING

Atchley, Robert C. *Social Forces in Later Life.* Belmont, Calif.: Wadsworth Publishing, 1980.

Provides an orientation to social gerontology and a summary of the impact of biological and psychological functioning. The book includes one section devoted to the situations that usually face aging individuals and another that discusses how society treats its older members. There is an instructor's manual with an annotated film guide.

Butler, Robert N. *Why Survive? Being Old in America.* New York: Harper and Row, 1977.

This book was written by the founder of the National Institute on Aging. It describes various studies on aging and its associated problems while exploring society's insensitivity to the needs of older people.

Haber, Carole. *Beyond Sixty-Five. The Dilemma of Old Age in America's Past.* Cambridge, England: Cambridge University Press, 1983.

Explores changes in the roles and perceptions of the elderly in America before the twentieth century, focusing on the creation of models of old age and superannuation that still influence our beliefs today.

Finkelhor, Dorothy. *The Triumph of Age.* Chicago: Follett, 1979.

Stresses that a retiree cannot solve the problems posed by this life transition with outdated attitudes. A retirement emotional quotient quiz helps determine one's emotional readiness for retirement.

Fromme, Alan. *Life After Work: Planning It. Living It. Loving It.* Glenview, Ill.: Scott, Foresman, 1984.

Emphasizes that a happy life after fifty is more a product of attitude than of opportunity or luck.

Keeton, Kathy. *Longevity: The Science of Staying Young.* New York: Viking, 1992.

"Getting old is no picnic, but it doesn't have to be a horror show either." With this positive attitude, the author explains in laymen's terms all the latest scientific trends in the study of aging. Keeton, president and founder of *Longevity* magazine, describes in detail her own strategies against aging, including anti-stress techniques, rejuvenation surgery, and dieting supplements. We all have the power to lengthen our lives, she believes, and some new approaches involve reducing food intake without sacrificing nutrition; lowering body temperature through meditation, self-hypnosis, and controlling the environment; and reexamining the roles of diet, sex, and exercise.

Kinzel, Robert K. *Retirement: Creating Promise Out of Threat.* New York: AMACOM, 1979.

The author, a retired management consultant, shows how retirees can analyze their lives to plan for productive retirement objectives.

Michaels, Joe. *Prime of Your Life.* New York: Quarto Marketing, 1981.

A guide for attaining individual fulfillment by reliance upon one's own values.

Tenenbaum, Frances. *Over 55 Is Not Illegal.* Boston: Houghton Mifflin, 1979.

A resource book on institutions, organizations, and agencies assisting active older adults. Offers advice on work, education, volunteer opportunities, and life satisfaction.

Uris, Auren. *Over 50: The Definitive Guide to Retirement.* Radnor, Pa.: Chilton, 1979.

An encyclopedia of preretirement issues, including transition from office to limbo, pensions, Social Security expectations, health and leisure planning, and men in retirement.

Weaver, Peter. *Strategies for the Second Half of Life.* New York: Franklin Watts, 1980.

Challenges preretirees to make the second half of life better than the first. Discusses second careers, health, financial planning, relationships, leisure, sex, and death.

CAREGIVING

Ball, Avis Jane. *Caring for an Aging Parent.* Buffalo, N.Y.: Prometheus Books, 1986.
A powerful account for families faced with the dilemma of parents who want to remain in familiar surroundings, yet are old, infirm, senile, or completely dependent on nursing care.

Buckingham, Robert W., Dr. P.H. *When Living Alone Means Living at Risk: A Guide for Caregivers and Families.* Buffalo, N.Y.: Prometheus Books, 1994.
This important book brings together an impressive array of authors who seek to assist family and friends in recognizing the danger signs that surround an at-risk elder, while making vital distinctions between those types of behavior that give cause for worry and those that can best be described as idiosyncratic. Caregivers and interested parties are offered suggestions for appropriate assistance that respects elder autonomy and freedom.

Fox, Nancy. *You, Your Parent and the Nursing Home: The Family's Guide to Long-Term Care.* Buffalo, N.Y.: Prometheus Books, 1986.
Anyone contemplating placing a parent in a nursing home knows that it is one of life's most difficult decisions. This book can help. The reader learns what to observe, during and after visiting hours. General nursing home practices, often considered "professional prerogatives," that may not contribute to the quality of care are disclosed. The author also shows how the family can be a positive influence on the care of elderly relatives.

Karr, Katherine L. *Taking Time for Me: How Caregivers Can Effectively Deal With Stress.* Buffalo, N.Y.: Prometheus Books, 1993.
Family caregivers often juggle their duties as parents and spouses with tending to the daily needs of a loved one who is elderly, chronically ill, or dying. As the cost of care forces many more people to assume the primary care needs of a family member, increasing numbers of care providers will become susceptible to high levels of anxiety and the physical as well as emotional stress it can bring. *Taking Time for Me* demonstrates that caregivers can overcome their personal conflicts and develop innovative ways of renewing their strength without jeopardizing the well-being of those

who depend on them. From exercise regimens and support groups to recognizing the humor in everyday situations, this book can revitalize caregivers for the challenges ahead.

Kenny, James, and Stephen Spicer. *Eldercare*. Buffalo, N.Y.: Prometheus Books, 1989.
This valuable book is useful for those who find themselves confronted with caring for an aging parent who is incapable of living alone. In practical and down-to-earth language, *Eldercare* demonstrates how to prepare your home for the arrival of an elder parent, how to plan programs of diet and exercise, or, if the need arises, how to choose a nursing home, and more. While the book maintains a compassionate tone, the authors do not overestimate the effort or level of dedication needed when caring for the elderly. Unlike other books on the subject of aging, this volume offers a "how to" approach to caring and a thoughtful explanation of the aging of both mind and body.

Rob, Caroline. *The Caregivers Guide*. Boston: Houghton Mifflin, 1991.
If you are stepping in to help an older relative or friend who can no longer manage alone with medical problems and daily living arrangements, this book provides information families need about medical concerns and where to go for help. It provides sensible, basic information: handling medical emergencies that strike the elderly, recognizing physical and mental problems, working with the latest medical advances for chronic disorders, keeping elders independent longer, and locating social services. This book makes clear that practical help can be found for every problem, so that the older person's days can be as active and enjoyable as possible, despite physical limitations.

FINANCIAL PLANNING

Baxter, Ralph C., Ph.D. *The Arthur Young Preretirement Planning Book*. New York: John Wiley & Sons, 1985.
This generalized overview of financial planning offers discussions on attitudes about aging, lifestyle, leisure time, second careers, health and safety, estate planning and legal matters. Includes a resources section on organizations, books, and films.

Clay, William C. *Dow Jones-Irwin Guide to Estate Planning.* 3rd ed. Homewood, Ill.: Dow Jones–Irwin, 1980.
A layman's guide to estate planning. Not a do-it-yourself plan, it presents information needed to secure professional assistance.

Hallman, V. G., and J. S. Rosenbloom. *Personal Financial Planning.* 3rd ed. New York: McGraw-Hill, 1982.
Concentrates on estate planning, Social Security, employer-provided retirement plans, and investment decisions people must make when approaching retirement.

Holden, Ronald R. *Estate Planning—A Family Affair Workbook.* Annapolis, Md.: Family Estate Planning Institute, 1986.
A workbook containing over twenty-two thought-provoking yet sensitive exercises, to be completed by both spouses, plus other planning tools to help a family face the complexities of estate planning.

Jorgensen, James. *The Graying of America.* New York: Dial Press, 1980.
A readable, knowledgeable analysis of the nation's pension plans. Examines Social Security, inflation, the baby boom, tax laws and weak pension legislation.

Lasser, J. K. *J. K. Lasser's Retirement Plan Handbook.* New York: J. K. Lasser Institute (updated yearly).
Provides clarification of the effect of income tax laws on the various types of retirement plans.

Parrott, William W., and John L. Parrott. *You Can Afford to Retire!* New York: New York Institute of Finance, 1992.
A systematic focus on all the key financial issues of planning a secure and comfortable retirement.

Rouse, Ken. *Putting Money in Its Place.* Boston: New England Financial Advisors, 1986.
Involves the reader effectively in a broad spectrum of basic considerations affecting the financial planning process, including defining what one wants in life, setting realistic goals, making the most of money to achieve those goals, and how to benefit from professional advisors.

Van Caspel, Venita. *The Power of Money Dynamics*. Reston, Va.: Prentice Hall, 1986.
A down-to-earth look at problems facing the investor today, with practical solutions to them.

Weaver, Peter, and Annette Buchanan. *What to Do with What You've Got*. Glenview, Ill.: Scott, Foresman, 1984.
Well-qualified authors stress the importance of learning how to manage financial resources to secure a comfortable retirement.

Weinstein, Grace. *Securing Your Retirement Dollars*. Washington, D.C.: American Council of Life Insurance—Health Insurance Association of America, 1984.
A comprehensive guide to financial planning, available free (1850 K St., NW, Washington, D.C. 20006).

GENERAL READING

Looking Ahead: How to Plan Your Successful Retirement. Washington, D.C.: American Association of Retired Persons, 1982.
A comprehensive overview, encouraging retirees to meet their retirement with confidence and a sense of discovery.

Berkinow, Louise. *Alone in America*. New York: Harper and Row, 1986.
A report on a pressing problem: loneliness. Explores the manifestations of this "disease" in the lives of executives, singles, gays and lesbians, senior citizens, widows and widowers, and families, reminding us that retirees are not alone with the problems of loneliness.

Biegel, Leonard. *The Best Years Catalogue*. New York: G. P. Putnam's Sons, 1978.
A comprehensive sourcebook of information on guidance services, publications, and bureaus that offer assistance to older people.

Comfort, Alex. *A Good Age*. New York: Simon & Schuster, 1976.
A vigorous, honest, well-written attack on the myths and stereotypes of aging that abound in American society.

Dickinson, Peter A. *The Complete Retirement Planning Book*. New York: E. P. Dutton, 1984.
A comprehensive guide by an author who has written widely on the subject. This expanded, revised edition offers updates on financial planning, housing, health and legal planning.

Downs, Hugh, and Richard J. Roll. *The Best Years Book*. New York: Delacorte Press, 1981.
An authoritative guide to planning for a vital, productive, and fulfilling retirement. It identifies issues and options and suggests strategies for making thoughtful plans.

Dunton, Loren. *The Vintage Years*. Berkeley, Calif.: Ten Speed Press, 1979.
A practical handbook offering both new and tried-and-true ideas about relating to grandchildren, decisions about wills, remarriage, and other retirement matters.

HEALTH

Baily, Covert. *Fit for Fat*. Boston: Houghton Mifflin, 1978.
A fitness book that summarizes recent research on diet, exercise and health maintenance. Written in a humorous style, it offers a readable, sensible approach.

Bortz, Walter M., II, M.D. *We Live Too Short and Die Too Long*. New York: Bantam, 1991.
Presents the best of the scientific research establishing that the natural life span the human body was designed to achieve is 120 years. Also outlines the basic practices people can begin today to age successfully.

Brody, Jane. *Good Food Book*. New York: W. W. Norton, 1985.
Already a classic on nutrition and fitness. The first part is a primer on the "new nutrition." The second part is a cookbook with over 350 recipes, plus menu plans.

Dardik, Irving, and Denis Waitley. *Quantum Fitness*. New York: Simon and Schuster, 1984.
Bonds the latest discoveries in psychology, nutrition, and exercise into a system to unlock each individual's maximum potential. Offers a three-part fitness and health program that anyone can follow.

D'Vries, Herbert A. *Vigor Regained*. Englewood Cliffs, N.J.: Prentice-Hall, 1974.
Outlines a simple, proven home program for restoring fitness and vitality in later years. Based on a research project conducted by D'Vries at Leisure World, California.

Farquhar, John W. *The American Way of Life Need Not Be Hazardous to Your Health*. New York: W. W. Norton, 1978.
Based on the Stanford Medical School Health Maintenance Plan, this book offers a plan for stress reduction and the development of a safe and sound exercise and nutrition program.

Fonda, Jane. *Women Coming of Age*. New York: Simon and Schuster, 1984.
Addresses the midlife physical concerns of women and provides a concrete program for midlife well-being.

Hallowell, Christopher. *Growing Old, Staying Young*. New York: William Morrow, 1985.
Explains the aging process and helps overcome the stereotypes surrounding the ills that beset many older people. Contains interviews with gerontologists and explains new research on aging.

Luce, Gay. *Your Second Life*. New York: Dell, 1979.
An insightful book that shatters old myths and suggests new attitudes toward aging, longevity, self-image, intimacy, sexuality, dreams, sleep, healing, and death.

Morgan, Robert F., and Jane Wilson. *Growing Younger: Adding Years to Your Life by Measuring and Controlling Your Body Age*. New York: Stein and Day, 1983.
This self-help book on how to measure one's body age outlines methods that can slow the aging process.

Ostrow, Andrew C. *Physical Activity and the Older Adult.* Princeton, N.J.: Princeton University Press, 1984.
The author, a physical education instructor, advocates the pursuit of physical activity, based on scientific research, throughout one's lifetime. Benefits include added vitality and a reduction of healthcare expenses.

Pelletier, Kenneth R. *Longevity: Fulfilling Our Biological Potential.* New York: Delacorte Press, 1981.
Applies the basic principles of holistic medicine and stresses reeducation about human longevity. Explores research links between longevity and the immune system, aging of cells, regeneration, exercise, diet, and mental attitudes.

HOUSING

Boyer, Richard, and David Savageau. *Places Rated Almanac.* Chicago: Rand McNally, 1985.
Ranks 329 metropolitan areas, comparing climate, housing, health, crime, transportation, education, the arts, recreation, and economic outlook.

Carlin, Vivian F., and Ruth Mansberg. *If I Live to Be 100: Congregate Housing for Later Life.* West Nyack, N.Y.: Parker Publishing, 1984.
The authors researched a middle-income congregate residence that typifies communal housing for older Americans. Their analysis may help those faced with complicated choices about where to live.

Dickinson, Peter A. *Retirement Edens outside the Sunbelt.* New York: E. P. Dutton, 1984.
A study of retirement housing options outside the Sunbelt areas. A look at staying put and how to design a housing situation to meet retirement needs in one's present home environment.

———. *Sunbelt Retirement.* New York: E. P. Dutton, 1984.
A comprehensive guide to successful retirement in each of the thirteen Sunbelt states. Each state, including over 500 cities and towns, is evaluated to offer practical answers to questions about cost of living, climate, healthcare, and lifestyle.

Down, Ivy M., and Lorraine Schnurr, Ph.D. *Between Home and Nursing Home: The Board and Care Alternative.* Buffalo, N.Y.: Prometheus Books, 1991.
For the elderly who do not require or cannot afford costly, full-time nursing care, board and care facilities may be a practical alternative. The majority of these homes accommodate from six to ten residents who are capable of some self-care but may need help with one or more basic activities of daily living.
This book offers information about this housing option, including what such homes are like and how they operate, how they are managed, what to look for when choosing a facility, how to monitor the care offered, what kinds of supervision and services should be available, and activities that contribute to residents' well-being.

Irwin, Robert. *The $100,000 Decision.* New York: McGraw Hill, 1981.
Treats the legal, financial, and psychological questions about selling a home, pocketing a tax-free bonanza, and choosing retirement housing.

Roper, Ann T. *National Continuing Care Directory.* Glenview, Ill.: Scott, Foresman, 1984.
A national consumer guide to help people locate a geographic area in which to retire. Describes the types of living arrangements and services offered by almost 300 continuing-care retirement communities.

Thomas, G. Scott. *The Rating Guide to Life in America's Small Cities.* Buffalo, N.Y.: Prometheus Books, 1990.
This study rates the quality of life in 219 cities with populations ranging from 15,000 to 50,000 residents in clearly defined statistical categories: climate/environment; recreation; economics; education; health care; housing; public safety; sophistication; transportation; and urban proximity.

Worley, Wilson H. *Retirement Living Alternatives USA. The Inside Story.* Clemson, S.C.: Columbia House, 1981.
Explains the pros and cons of the varying concepts about retirement living learned in a five-year study of living options. Summarizes interviews with five thousand retirees.

LEGAL ISSUES

Daly, Eugene J. *Thy Will Be Done: A Guide to Wills, Taxation, and Estate Planning for Older Persons.* Rev. ed. Amherst, N.Y.: Prometheus Books, 1994.
Written specifically for older persons who want to put their estates in order, this book answers the questions most often asked about wills, inheritances, trusts, protecting assets from taxation, how to choose an executor, amending a will, and much more. Includes money-saving suggestions, examples, a glossary of terms, and a sample will.

Kess, S., and B. Weslin. *Estate Planning Guide.* Chicago: Commerce Clearing House, 1982.
Designed to aid the estate owner and his/her advisors in the formulation of a successful estate plan. Analyzes planning techniques and principles for executives, professionals and partners, owners of an interest in closed corporations, sole proprietors, and single women.

National Insurance Consumer Organization. *Buyer's Guide to Insurance: What the Companies Won't Tell You.* Alexandria, Va., undated.
Reveals facts not commonly known about the various kinds of insurance. Designed to assist consumers in making more informed choices among insurance options.

Soldad, Alex J. *The Essential Guide to Wills, Estates, Trusts and Death Taxes.* Glenview, Ill.: Scott, Foresman, 1984.
This guide, published by the American Association of Retired Persons, explains in layman's terms the various legal concepts involved and the absolute necessity for advance planning.

Wishard, William R. *Rights of the Elderly and Retired.* San Francisco: Cragmont Publications, 1978.
A comprehensive guide to legal rights and issues that may come into question at retirement. Included is information about retirement benefits (public and private), health and medical services, housing, employment, age discrimination, and consumer rights and protection.

LEISURE

Bodkin, Cora; Helene Leibowitz; and Diana Wiener. *Crafts for Your Leisure Years.* Boston: Houghton Mifflin, 1976.
Contains twenty-five specially designed projects with step-by-step instructions.

McMillon, Bill. *Volunteer Vacations: A Directory of Short-Term Adventures That Will Benefit You and Others.* Chicago: Chicago Review Press, 1991.
Here are detailed accounts of more than 190 organizations that sponsor over two thousand projects throughout the year, ranging from one to six weeks long, at a wide range of costs. Included are anecdotes and photographs from people who have taken many kinds of volunteer vacations, offering readers a glimpse of the challenges, personal growth, and fun that await them. Indexes enable the reader to narrow myriad options according to how much time and money is available, location interests, and the reader's skills and interests.

RELATIONSHIPS

Dodson, F. *How to Grandparent.* New York: Harper and Row, 1981.
A guide to contemporary grandparenting and the need to understand changes and their effect on grandparents, children, and grandchildren. Topics include discipline, working mothers, divorce, single children, gifts, and visits.

Finkelhor, Dorothy. *The Liberated Grandmother.* New York: Prince Communications, 1979.
A contemporary nontraditional approach to grandmothering. The author shows women how to love grandchildren yet attain self-realization through freedom of action, thought, and emotion.

Fogel, Robert W.; Elaine Hatfield; Sara B. Kiesler; and Ethel Shanas. *Aging: Stability and Change in the Family.* New York: Academic Press, 1981.
Contains writings and research findings by seventeen gerontologists and social and behavioral scientists. It explores facets of family relationships as they are altered and influenced by aging.

Hyman, Helen Kandel, and Barbara Silverstone. *Growing Older Together: A Couple's Guide to Understanding and Coping with the Challenges of Later Life*. New York: Pantheon, 1992.
Takes couples over fifty-five through the unique terrain of later life: the myriad practical and emotional hurdles that must be overcome so that husbands and wives can meet the challenges of old age.

Mace, Nancy, and Peter Rapins. *The 36-Hour Day*. New York: Warner, 1981.
A family guide to caring for persons with Alzheimer's disease.

Shahan, L. *Living Alone and Liking It*. New York: Harper and Row, 1981.
Living techniques for the widowed, separated, and divorced to help them discover that life on their own can be full, free, and exciting.

Shelley, Florence D. *When Your Parents Grow Old*. New York: Harper and Row, 1988.
This updated edition of the standard reference work by Florence D. Shelley and Jane Otten is devoted to improving the quality of a parent's life, including housing options, home care, choosing a nursing home, health, and behavioral changes.

Silverstone, Barbara, and Helen Hyman. *You and Your Aging Parent*. New York: Pantheon, 1982.
Reviews financial and medical assistance available to those over sixty-five. Describes community services that offer alternatives to nursing home care, and contains a listing of state and local agencies available to assist families.

Slaybaugh, Charles S. *The Grandparents' Catalog: An Idea Book for Family Sharing*. Mogadore, Ohio: Slaybaugh and Associates, 1984.
A big book filled with ideas on how grandparents and their grandchildren can enjoy each other, grow together, and help strengthen family ties.

SECOND CAREERS

Bird, Caroline. *Second Careers: New Ways to Work After 50*. Boston: Little, Brown, 1992.
Based on the *Modern Maturity* magazine survey, this book addresses the many issues concerning our changing attitudes about our work lives as it analyzes the career switches of more than six thousand people in nearly three hundred occupations.

Deichman, Elizabeth S., Ed.M., and Regina Kociekci. *Working with the Elderly: An Introduction*. Buffalo, N.Y.: Prometheus Books, 1989.
Written in response to educators' requests for just such a book, this is the most comprehensive work available for those considering a career in the growing field of gerontology. Areas of opportunity in the physical, psychological, environmental, legal, ethical, and health professions are described by practitioners who possess broad experience and who share the goal of responsible, effective service. Also provided are historical and political perspectives on emerging issues in gerontology.

France, Van Arsdale. *Career Planning for Senior Adults*. Lake Forest, Calif.: J & U Publications, 1980.
Explores career options, counseling techniques to assist mature adults in planning for second careers.

SEX

Brecher, Edward M. *Love, Sex and Aging*. Boston: Little, Brown, 1984.
A comprehensive study of sexual attitudes and activities of Americans over fifty. Assembled from responses of 4,246 men and women to detailed questionnaires, it contains practical information and advice on sexuality in later years.

Butler, Robert N., and Myrna Lewis. *Sex After Sixty: A Guide for Men and Women in Their Later Years*. New York: Harper and Row, 1976.
This sensitive work about the sexual lives of men and women over sixty studies the sexual difficulties that can arise at this time of

life, with emphasis on the "how to" of building a warm and mutually satisfying sexual relationship in later years.

Hammond, Doris B., Ph.D. *My Parents Never Had Sex.* Buffalo, N.Y.: Prometheus Books, 1987.
Did your parents have sex? Many young adult children have a hard time thinking of their parents as sexual beings. And older persons harbor erroneous views of what is sexually appropriate for people "their age." This volume presents straightforward facts about sexual aging, providing a positive impression of elders as sexual beings.

Peterson, James A., and Barbara Payne. *Love in the Later Years.* New York: Association Press, 1975.
An effort to help the older adult become aware of his or her potential in any loving relationship. Among the topics covered are marriages and life in later years, retirement marriage, emerging innovations in lifestyles, the economics of later marriage, and planning for the future.

Weg, Ruth B. *Sexuality in the Later Years.* New York: Academic Press, 1983.
Using evidence from many disciplines, the author presents a total picture of sexual roles and behavior in the later years.

TRAVEL

Dickinson, Peter A. *Travel and Retirement Edens Abroad.* Larchmont, N.Y.: Dickinson Publishing, 1984.
A comprehensive description of travel and living destinations outside the United States that have popular appeal for American retirees.

WOMEN IN RETIREMENT/SINGLES

Jacobs, Ruth. *Life After Youth: Female, Forty—What's Next?* Scranton, Pa.: Harper and Row, 1979.
A sensible, sympathetic and informal look at the older women of today. Suggests liberating roles for women in their later years, translating past experiences into new roles.

Kehoe, Monika. Ph.D. *Lesbians over 60 Speak for Themselves.* Binghamton, N.Y.: The Haworth Press, 1990.
This pioneering effort is the first attempt to reach a nationwide representation of lesbian elders in order to understand this deeply hidden segment of our population. These women candidly describe their necessarily secret lives in a hostile society, how they feel about being "different," their most pressing problems, how aging has affected them, and their sexual behavior—as it was in their youth and as it is now.

Seskin, Jane. *More Than Mere Survival: Conversations with Women over 65.* New York: Newsweek Books, 1980.
Twenty-two women between the ages of sixty-six and ninety-seven reveal how much joy, interest, and pleasure they find in their lives—and how they found it. Despite their physical disabilities, economic hardships, or loss of family and friends, each has preserved a zest for living, self-confidence, and sense of humor.

Szinovacz, Maximiliane. *Women's Retirement: Policy Implications of Recent Research.* Beverly Hills: Sage Publications, 1982.
Discusses the female experience of adjusting to retirement. Topics include employment status, living situations, attitudes, and planning.

Thorne, Ruth Raymond. *Women and Aging: Celebrating Ourselves.* Binghamton, N.Y.: The Haworth Press, 1992.
This is a valuable guide to help women break through the negative stereotypes of old age and find personal fulfillment through the stages of maturity. Full of warmth and support, *Women and Aging* enables women to take and remain in control of their lives instead of passively letting others make life-changing and possibly harmful decisions for them. This essential guide for aging will help women increase the vitality of their old age, as it urges them to continue to plan for the future, keep and develop strong re-

lationships, increase their overall wellness, and not be afraid to take risks.

Troll, Lillian E. *Looking Ahead: A Woman's Guide to the Problems and Joys of Growing Older.* Englewood Cliffs, N.J.: Prentice Hall, 1977.

Reviews a variety of aspects of aging as it applies to women. A collection of some of the first thinking on the issues of the sociology of the aging of women, retirement, parent-child relationships, friendships, education, marriage, and widowhood.

Postscript

Retirement really can be an adventure with thoughtful and thorough planning. In this book I have tried to present those issues that I have found to be most important to a successful retirement experience, concentrating on quality of life after retirement and an awareness of healthy, life-prolonging behaviors and lifestyles.

Because my research comes in large part from real people and their current retirement experiences, I am always seeking out older people to talk to as I travel around the country. I have struck up conversations in airports, at cocktail parties, in elevators, during business functions, and even at weddings. I ask people about their lives and what, if anything, they would change about retirement. What were the surprises they had not anticipated, both good and bad? I am always curious about what advice they want to pass along to preretirees. I always learn something new!

Retirement can be such an extraordinary time, while uniquely personal. I would like to invite you, the reader, to write and tell me about your retirement experience. Let me know if you planned ahead of time and how, including any mistakes you made and what you might have done differently. If there are things you discovered that you think others would be interested in, or any advice you would like to share with people not yet retired, please pass that on.

I look forward to hearing from you. Please write to me in care of the publisher—and enjoy your retirement!

Thank you.

Guild A. Fetridge